JESUS LOVES THE CHURCH
AND SO SHOULD YOU

This book is
given to Zac & Hannah
Turkman
with blessings

from
Gramma
Calhoun
Sept '16

Earl Michael Blackburn

Upon completion of his theological education, Earl labored in Utah for seven years as a church planting missionary carrying the gospel to the Mormons. He has been in the ordained ministry for 35 years and has traveled extensively preaching in Pastors' Conferences in Europe, Africa, and Asia. He has contributed to the book *Denominations or Associations* (Calvary Press, 2001), has written for a number of magazines, and has authored several booklets. As a cancer survivor, he now pastors Heritage Baptist Church, a rebuilding inner-city work in Shreveport, Louisiana. He and his wife Debby have been married since 1975 and have one son Caleb.

Words of High Praise for *Jesus Loves the Church and So Should You*

"Earl Blackburn's much-needed *Jesus Loves the Church and So Should You* is scripturally rich and timely, and succinct yet thorough. His chapters on church membership are superlative. This book should be read by every Christian particularly in our day when love for Christ's bride, the church, is on the wane. I would recommend that every church give a copy of this book to each church family and encourage group studies on it. Who can tell what God will do with such a book as this?" - **Joel R. Beeke**, PhD., Puritan Reformed Theological Seminary, Grand Rapids, MI

"I am impressed with the scope, depth, relevance, biblical fidelity, and infectious spiritual fervor of Earl Blackburn's *Jesus Loves the Church, and So Should You*. Every pastor should lead a congregational study of this book; he should make this a priority for the health of the body itself, and personal growth of each person in the membership. Blackburn has dealt with an amazing number of questions concerning church membership, church purpose, the nature of the church, the functioning of a church, how and why to leave a church, how not to leave a church, why be a church member and what to expect a church to be. All of his discussions [short, pithy, clear, engaging discussions] are settled firmly on Scripture and illustrated through well-selected citations from some of the most spiritually-minded fathers of Christian history. Naught but good could come from engaging the entire church in a determined, week-by-week, reading and discussion of the principles to which Pastor Blackburn has given such expert exposition." - **Tom Nettles**, PhD., The Southern Baptist Theological Seminary, Louisville, KY

"This book deals with important questions regarding the church and church membership. It is a timely book. In our day, many tend to view the church as an institution that almost anyone can join, where there are few expectations and little accountability. In contrast, Earl Blackburn presents the Biblical truth that the church is a living organism intended to reflect the life of our Lord in its membership. You will be blessed, enriched and challenged as you explore this carefully researched work." - **Wayne DuBose**, Director of Missions, Northwest Louisiana Baptist Association

"Earl Blackburn loves the church of Jesus Christ, but better than that, he loves it intelligently and scripturally. Written by a true churchman for those who want to honor Christ in His own house." - **Robert P. Martin**, PhD., Pastor of Emmanuel Reformed Baptist Church, Seattle, WA

"It is with the voice of thanksgiving that I commend Pastor Earl Blackburn's *Jesus Loves the Church and So Should You*. There is a warm recognition of the love of Christ for each of His individual sheep all the way through the book. But, with biblical clarity, Pastor Blackburn shines the light of Christ's love on His church, both universal and local. This latter emphasis is just what is needed by professing Christians all over the world, but especially in America. The rugged individualism and emphasis upon personal freedom in our country has seeped into the mentality of American Christians so as to diminish the importance in their thinking of belonging to and being faithful to a local church. Yet Christ and His Apostles have made it clear that the local church is the authorized outpost of Christ's kingdom designed by Him to order His worship, to edify His sheep, and to take His gospel to the ends of the earth. Individual sheep must learn to love Christ's fold as He does... His local church.

Pastor Blackburn has provided two major things for Christians to understand: (1) what the Scripture says is a biblical church; and (2) how the Christian should respond to the will of Jesus Christ in their church membership. Various errors in thinking about the purpose and membership of a local church are well delineated and answered from Scripture. Building a sound biblical theology of the church, the author proceeds to well-stated and clear applications to the Christian's proper attitude toward and commitment to a local church.

This book challenges both pastor and people to have the same attitude toward the church that our dear Lord has as Head of each one. For Christ loved the church and gave Himself up for her...and so should we. The great strength of this book is that Pastor Blackburn says what every pastor wants his people to understand about loving Christ's church. For this reason, I commend this book as a spark to light the fire of biblical reformation today beyond agreement to "the doctrines of grace" to their end: to bring forth a people who love Christ and love one another...in the church." - **Fred Malone**, PhD., Pastor of First Baptist Church, Clinton, LA

"Pastoral, Christ-like love for the church shines forth in this book by a dear servant of God. Anyone who has met Earl Blackburn knows the message of this book flows from the center of his heart. May this book serve to kindle afresh within the hearts of God's people a deep love for His church." - **Ray Van Neste**, Ph.D., Associate Professor of Christian Studies, Director, R. C. Ryan Center for Biblical Studies, Union University, Jackson, TN

"The church is under siege by an abundance of bad ideas. This book is a must read in our day. It is a whetstone to hone the edge of a sharpened sword preparing the Christian soldier for this spiritual battlefront." - **Mike Renihan**, PhD., Pastor of Heritage Baptist Church, Worcester, MA

"I have known Earl for 30 years, during which time we have struggled together making decisions, studied hard to advance our scholarship in the gospel, endured the inevitable problems arising from pastoral ministry, and depended upon one another for honest counsel; agreeing with him most of the time and finding it to have been profitable when we did not. He is a serious student, excels in his grasp of technical and controversial matters, and is gifted and tireless in his efforts to pass this on to faithful men. It is my privilege to be known as one of the 'Rowdy Friends' he mentions in his Preface. His love for Christ's church is known far beyond my slender recommendation. I can commend without reserve this his latest work on a subject dear to his heart." - **Tom Lyon**, Pastor of Providence Reformed Baptist Church, University Place, WA

"Having known and worked with Pastor Earl Blackburn for many years, I have repeatedly seen his love for Christ and local congregations. His insight and cogent thinking regarding practical ecclesiology have been a repeated help to me as a pastor of two Reformed Baptist churches. Many believers have been helped by his instruction concerning these things in the material he has previously written. I'm very pleased to see his booklets brought together in one work, expanded and improved by the serious study and mature reflection of our dear brother. I believe this book will be of invaluable help to the dear people of Christ's Church who read it and follow the godly wisdom expressed in it." - **Larry Vincent**, Pastor of Heritage Baptist Church, Mansfield, TX

Jesus Loves the Church
And So Should You

Studies in Biblical Churchmanship

Earl M. Blackburn

Solid Ground Christian Books
Birmingham, Alabama USA

Solid Ground Christian Books
PO Box 660132
Vestavia Hills AL 35266
205-443-0311
mike.sgcb@gmail.com
www.solid-ground-books.com

JESUS LOVES THE CHURCH AND SO SHOULD YOU
Studies in Biblical Churchmanship

by Earl M. Blackburn

First Edition November 2010

Cover image is taken from a photo by Ric Ergenbright
of a church in Hallstatt, Salzburg Lake District, Austria.

Cover design by Borgo Design
Contact them at borgogirl@bellsouth.net

ISBN- 978-159925-249-0

PREFACE

Every major systematic theology has a section covering ecclesiology or the doctrine of the church. Also, there are many excellent, scholarly books dealing with this subject on an enrichingly deep level. However, this book is not one of them, nor is it intended to be. It is not for the "groves of academia," but for the average person, who has given little thought to the nature of a biblical church or membership in one. I have purposely written it for a practical and entry-level study of biblical churchmanship. Though written from a Baptist position to help Baptist churches, it is also intended to benefit the broader evangelical community. Each chapter is designed to be read as an independent study. Some chapters contain a slight degree of repetition; this is to reinforce objective truth. Ultimately, my desired end is for you to see how much Christ loved, and still loves, the church and for you to love and be an active member of one of Christ's churches.

There are several people I wish to thank:

All my "rowdy friends," who have lightened the load and enriched my journey. You know who you are;

"Miss" Nancy, who keeps telling me "Keep it simple, Bro. Earl";

Paul, my fellow elder, who is more of a "Paul" than he realizes;

Casey, our pastoral intern, a "Timothy" indeed; who has caused me to see that there is a younger generation who passionately esteems the church and theology;

Holly, a philologist, who has lovingly and painstakingly "bloodied" my numerous drafts with her red pen. May her kind increase;

Caleb, my "mainest man in the wholest world" (not good English, but expressive of my heart). May he ever love Christ and His house;

Debby, my precious Sweetheart and "life's best companion" (to quote Calvin of Idelette), since 1974, when she first stole my heart. What and where would I be without her? Truly, her "price is far above rubies";

And Christ, the glorious second Person of the Godhead, whose eternal love for me has caused me to love Him, His Word, and His church. Worthy is the stem of Jesse, the Lord our righteousness, the Lamb and Lion of the tribe of Judah!

Earl M. Blackburn
Bossier City, Louisiana
October, 2010

TABLE OF CONTENTS

INTRODUCTION

"...and upon this rock I will build my church; and the gates of hell shall not prevail against it." (Matthew 16:18)

IN OUR POSTMODERN SOCIETY, certain words are sure to provoke discussion and, often, an unpopular response. "Church" and "church membership" are two examples. Before reacting negatively to them, however, the reader should give careful attention to these significant and weighty subjects. The Bible has much to say about church and church membership that will, if heeded, strengthen the Christian's life and worship.

The realm of church membership generally includes five groups of people. The **first** group consists of those who think the church is nothing more than a social club and joining it is no different than joining any other civic organization for enhancing a person's status in society. This is because many churches have departed from orthodox Christian doctrine and have become institutions of men. Assuming they began well, they ceased following the Word of God and began following cunningly devised fables and traditions of men (2 Peter 1:16), which caused Christ to remove His presence. They are churches in name only.

Second, among those who love God's Word and have saving faith in the Lord Jesus Christ, there is the attitude that the church and church membership is unimportant or even divisive. Many believers say, "All that's really important is that I belong to the universal church, which is His body. I don't need the visible church or to be a member of a particular congregation." They tell church leaders, "I want to be free to worship where I want, when I want, without the legalism of church membership." This group believes there is no such teaching in the Bible as "church membership." Sadly, this attitude is widespread.

The **third** group consists of those who are church members and do not know why. After their profession of faith, someone suggested that it would be a good thing to find a church and join it. So, they went to a church building, talked with a church leader, and requested church membership. On the next Sunday, they were promptly received into membership without knowing anything of the true nature of a church or of biblical church membership. Often, they attend for a few weeks, drop out, and seldom return to church except for Christmas and Easter. Yet, their names remain on the membership roll, though they have no commitment or active participation in the life of the church.

The **fourth** group is those who are cultural church members. These are they whose parents were members of a church and from the day of their birth, they have been in the same church or denomination. In some situations, five and six generations of their family have been members of the same church. To *not* be a member of a church or to *not* attend on a regular basis is unthinkable. Yet, they are members, not by conversion to Christ, but by familial and cultural tradition. As an old witticism goes, "They are Baptist born, and Baptist bred, and when they die, they'll be Baptist dead." (You can substitute any other denomination to fit the saying.) There is a close-minded sense of ownership in the church (i.e., "This is my church."), but no genuine love for the church.

The four previously mentioned positions must be avoided at all costs! There is, however, a *fifth* group. These people understand the importance and implications of the scriptural teaching upon the subject of the church and have sought to conform themselves to it. An active participation in the church and biblical churchmanship is their joy and delight. The love of Christ constrains them and they find His commands are not grievous (John 14:15; cf. 1 John 5:3). To these people, keeping the precepts of Christ their Savior and Lord is exhilarating. The benefits and practical advantages they experience are life-changing. It is important, then, to understand and to be a part of this company. Therefore, let it be clear to the reader that the design of this book is to incite and to encourage you to love the church as Jesus loves it and to implement biblical church-manship in your life.

DISCUSSION FOR THE INTRODUCTION:

1. Why do you think words such as "church" and "church membership" often provoke negative responses?

2. What are the five groups of people and their attitudes toward being a member of a church?

3. Which of these groups best describes your personal attitude and practice?

4. Do you think it is important to be a part of the fifth group? Why?

1

JESUS LOVED AND STILL LOVES THE CHURCH

*"Husbands, love your wives,
even as Christ also loved the church and gave himself for it."*
(Ephesians 5:25)

WHAT A BEAUTIFUL STATEMENT Paul the Apostle made when he emphatically declared—*"Christ also loved the church and gave Himself for it."* Here is described the Lord of heaven, the One who was face to face with God, and who, before there was ever a beginning, *was*. It is He whom the seraphim praised, who is the express character and brightness of the Father's glory and the second Person of the Trinity, who left the world of adoration and light and came into this world of cursing and darkness. He became one of us and one with us, the God-in-fleshed Man who lived and walked among us. Why did He come? For what purpose? With what intent? The one defining, inerrantly-given answer is—love. But, we ask, love for what? Without any equivocation, Paul tells us—the church. Love was the powerful, compelling force that moved Jesus from heaven to earth, and the purchase of the church was His goal. Jesus loved the church.

Jesus' love for the church is not just an emotional, mystical cliché to be tossed around with little meaning. His love was demonstrated and can be seen in a real, tangible way. He came to build the church (Matthew 16:18). He founded it while on the earth (Matthew 16:18, 18:17) in the calling of that noble apostolic band of Twelve. The church is seen here in embryo form as, for three years, Jesus instructed and trained them to lay a foundation in which He would be the chief cornerstone (Ephesians 2:20). He lovingly lived a life of perfect obedience to His Father's holy Law so that His beloved ones might have imputed to them a perfect righteousness that allows them *safe* entrance into heaven. The highest expression of that love is seen on the cross, when great David's greater Son, the God-man, sacrificed Himself and purchased the church with His own blood (Acts 20:28). What wondrous love is this, O my soul?

What words give a biblical description of how Jesus loved the church? The following adverbs and verses teach us something about this question:

Jesus loved the church *eternally.* His arrival in Bethlehem, via the womb of a virgin, did not just happen by luck or chance. Before the worlds began in the eternal council of redemption, the Father gave Jesus a particular number of people (that is later called the church) to be special objects of His love.[1]

Aimlessness was not part of the Savior's agenda. He *intentionally* loved the church; nothing would deter Him from going to the cross to purchase His church. Love is seen driving Him as He *"set His face like a flint"* toward Jerusalem and a meeting with destiny—crucifixion (Luke 9:51; cf. Isaiah 50:7).

When we had nothing to offer God but our sin, when we were enemies of His Law and grace (Romans 5:8), and when we were *"children of wrath even as others"* (Ephesians 2:3b), Christ loved us, His

---

[1] e.g., John 6:37, 10:10-11, 14-17 & 25-30, 15:9, 17:9 & 23-24; Ephesians 1:4-6; Romans 8:29-30 (note that "foreknew" in v. 29 means, in the original language of the NT, "foreloved").

church, **unconditionally**. There were no strings attached to His love. He does not love us one day and hate us the next. On the best of our days and the worst, the Savior loves us without condition.

Everything Jesus did was a continual sacrifice of Himself to do the will of the Father (Hebrews 10:9-10; cf. Isaiah 40:7-8). Once He commenced His ministry at the age of thirty, He had no permanent, earthly residence. He could humbly say, in contrast to those who hesitated in doing the will of God, *"Foxes have holes and birds of the air have nests, but the Son of Man has nowhere to lay His head"* (Matthew 8:20). His entire life was a living sacrifice to His Father and His God. This is never seen so clearly as when on the cross, He *"gave Himself"* **sacrificially** for the church.

With intense joy Jesus instituted the Lord's Supper in the upper room on the night in which he was betrayed (Luke 22:14-23), revealing how **affectionately** He loved the church. The Apostle John opens the *Upper Room Discourse* of John 13-17 with these words, *"Now before the Feast of the Passover, when Jesus knew that His hour had come that He should depart from this world to the Father, having loved His own who were in the world, He loved them to the end."* In the last few hours before His decease, Jesus tenderly and affectionately taught the apostles, the "pillars" of the church.

Above all that Jesus loved, the church was His supreme delight. He loved the church **chiefly**, as Paul revealed in Ephesians 5:25. He prized her as His bride, as a husband would his betrothed above all other women.

Will Jesus ever stop loving the church? Will He one day consider her to be outdated or no longer useful? Will He relegate her to the archives of antiquity? No, a thousand times, no! Throughout all the ages of eternity, Christ shall love the church **endlessly** as His blood-washed Bride (Revelation 7:9-17).

Christ not only loved the church, but He *still* loves the church. He actively cherishes and adores, nourishes and feeds, protects and defends, purifies and makes holy the church (Ephesians 5:25-27). He faithfully prays and intercedes for His church (Hebrews 7:25-27; 1 John 2:1) and is her *only* Head (Ephesians 5:23; Colossians 1:18). Above all, the Lord Jesus Christ is in the midst of His churches. When John saw Him as the glorified and reigning Lord (Revelation 1:13), where was Christ standing and what was He doing? He was standing among the lampstands, which are His churches. In addition, He was holding seven stars in His right hand, which are the *"angels,"* or messengers (pastors), of His churches (v. 13a, 16a, & 20). He speaks to His churches via His messengers (Revelation 2:1, 8, 12, 18; 3:1, 7 & 14). Furthermore, He continually interacts and teaches His churches with plain directives, fearful warnings, and exhilarating promises (Revelation 2:6, 9, 16, 24; 3:2, 8 & 18-19). Jesus *still* loves the church. Since Jesus still loves the church, should you not also love it?

DISCUSSION FOR CHAPTER ONE:

1. What are the descriptions of Christ mentioned in the first two paragraphs of this chapter?

2. How do we know from Scripture that Jesus' love was not merely an emotional, mystical cliché?

3. Discuss the seven adverbial words that tell how Christ loved the church.

4. What scriptural evidence is there that Jesus *still* loves the church?

5. Are you a Christian? Do you love the church? How can you say you love Christ if you do not love the thing on the earth that He loves chiefly?

2

THE NEW TESTAMENT IS A CHURCH BOOK

". . . besides the other things, what comes upon me daily:
my deep concern for all the churches."
(2 Corinthians 11:28)

MOST CHRISTIANS THINK that the books of the New
Testament (NT) were written to individual believers. They read
their Bibles, seldom thinking beyond their own personal life
experiences. As the old saying goes, "They do not see the forest
because of the trees." There is a massive failure to realize to
whom the bulk of the NT was written. To whom were the
majority of the twenty-seven (27) books of the NT written?
Apart from the historical books of the Gospels and Acts, the
vast majority was written to visible bodies of Christ—churches.
Others, not directly written to churches, were written to leaders
of churches, instructing them how to lead and govern their
congregations. Even those *few* remaining books, that do not
deal directly with local churches or church leaders, *indirectly* have
numerous references to churches—assemblies, congregations,
bodies, etc., (Hebrews 10:25; James 2:2; 1 Peter 4:17; 3 John 10).
The NT knows nothing of a churchless Christianity.

When the word "church" (*ekklesia*) is used in the NT, it
overwhelmingly refers to visible congregations. The **first** time
the word is used, it denotes a confessional body (Matthew

16:18); the **second** time it is used, it denotes a disciplinary body (Matthew 18:15-20). Of the *114* times the Greek word *ekklesia* is inerrantly written, *three* times it speaks of a secular gathering (Acts 19:32, 39 & 41). Only *five* times[2] does the word refer to the universal body of Christ. Even these *five* carry the idea of community, especially as they are gathered in heaven (e.g., Hebrews 12:23). In the remaining *106* times the word is used (ninety-six percent), it refers to visible congregations of baptized believers.

The New Testament is a "church" book. Consider the following:

- The Book of Acts is replete with references to the church (2:47, 11:22, 12:5, 13:1-3, 14:26-28, et al).

- The Book of Romans was written to the churches in Rome (1:7).

- The Books of 1 & 2 Corinthians were written to the church in Corinth (1:2 & 1:1).

- The Book of Galatians was written to churches in Galatia (1:2).

- The Book of Ephesians was written to the church in Ephesus (1:1).

- The Book of Philippians was written to the church in Philippi (1:1), with its bishops and deacons.

---

2 See Matthew 16:18; Ephesians 1:22-23, 3:10; Colossians 1:18; and Hebrews 12:23. Since the Ephesians and Colossians verses were written to visible churches, some would argue that these verses refer to visible churches rather than to the universal body of Christ.

- The Book of Colossians was written to the three churches in the Lycus Valley: Colosse, Hierapolis, and Laodicea (4:13-16).

- The Books of 1 & 2 Thessalonians were written to the church in Thessalonica (1:1 & 1:1).

- The Books of 1 & 2 Timothy were written to a young pastor (1:1). Church History tells us Timothy was eventually the pastor of the church of Ephesus.

- The Book of Titus was written to a church leader in Crete (1:4-5).

- The Book of Philemon was written to a pastor of a large "house church" (1-2).

- The Book of Hebrews refers to *"assembling...together"* (10:25), which is a formal, liturgical word that denotes only church worship. Also, the Hebrews writer refers to those *"who have spoken the Word of God"* (13:7) and who have *"rule"* over the church (13:17).

- The Book of James deals with showing preferential treatment to the rich over the poor who come into the church assembly (2:2).

- The Books of 1 & 2 Peter refer to "judgment beginning in the house of God" (4:17-18), meaning the church.

- The Books of 1, 2, & 3 John have churchly references (1 John 2:19, *"they went out from us. . ."*; 3 John 6, *"who have borne witness before the church"*; 3 John 9-10, warns of an authoritarian leader, who loved to have the preeminence and abusively *"put"* humble brethren out of the church).

- The Book of Jude speaks of *"love feasts,"* which historically were communion celebrations of the church (12).

- The Book of Revelation was not written, as some mistakenly suppose, to the church in the 21st century, but to seven visible churches in Asia Minor (chapters 1-3). If it had been written *only* for us today, it would have had no meaning or significance for those churches in the first century.

What pattern do we see here? Simply stated, the NT is a church book. If you remove the church and all its varied aspects from the NT, you have virtually no NT at all.

DISCUSSION FOR CHAPTER TWO:

1. Why do you suppose many believers think of the NT only in individual terms?

2. To whom was the bulk of the NT books written?

3. How many times is the Greek word for church found in the NT? How many times does the word refer to visible churches (i.e., congregations)? Why do you think this is so?

4. Do you think it is correct to speak of the NT as a "church" book? Why or why not?

5. What would you have if you were to remove the teachings about the church from the NT?

3

WHAT IS THE CHURCH?
CHURCH UNIVERSAL AND CHURCH VISIBLE

"These things I write to you, though I hope to come to you shortly;
but if I am delayed, I write so that you may know how you ought to conduct
yourself in the house of God, which is the church of the living God,
the pillar and ground of truth."
(1 Timothy 3:14-15)

THERE IS WIDESPREAD confusion, both in the world and in Christianity, regarding the nature and identity of the church. What is a church? Is it a building? Is it the body of ordained clergy? Is it the universal body of believers in Christ through all ages? Is it a religious worship service? Is it a denomination or a group of churches? Is it simply a group of believers in Christ? Everyone who uses the word "church" does not have the same understanding.

The state of the church, as a whole, is in horrible disrepair. Its walls need rebuilding much like the walls of Jerusalem in Nehemiah's day. There is mass disaffection with biblical ecclesiology. It is often said, "We don't need to worry about church order; let's get on with reaching people." A Protestant form of Jesuitism,[3] which says "the end justifies the means," has

---

[3] Jesuits - a Roman Catholic society formed in 1534 by Ignatius Loyola primarily to counter and stamp out the Protestant Reformation. Its philosophy has always been

settled into 21st century evangelicalism. As long as it appears the church is growing and the results of reaching people are seemingly accomplished, many Christians are happy.

In numerous cases, there is a careless re-structuring of the biblical ecclesiastical system. There is an accumulation of unbiblical offices and positions that bypass divine order (e.g., trustees, stewards, committees, boards, etc.). In other cases, there is a wholesale abandonment of the church, a view that the church is unimportant. The church is *not* needed because "I'm saved and that's all that matters." In still other cases, there is the mindset that the church has failed and has outlived its usefulness. It is a relic that must be confined to the archives of yesteryear.

There is also the proliferation of para-church organizations, thought by many to be absolutely necessary. The use of "para" indicates or suggests something that is "beside" or "alongside." Walt Chantry precisely makes the following observation:

> Too many individuals and activists have had a 'better idea' than the church. With disparaging remarks about the weaknesses, failures, and inefficiencies of the church, movements are begun 'beside' the church. Claims are made that such persons or agencies are working 'alongside' the church, stressing that their efforts are 'parallel' to and 'supportive' of the church. However, that which is 'alongside' is still 'outside' the church. How zealous and self-promoting are such para-church organizations. Para-church works can only justify their existence by criticism of the church. How different this is from our Lord's concept of missions and evangelism which builds up the church.[4]

---

to use deceit, dissimulation, immorality, even adultery and murder, or any other means available, to accomplish its purposes.

[4] *Missionaries Should Be "Immersed" In The Church*, (Carlisle, PA: Reformed Baptist Publication, nd).

What is the true nature of the church? While much has been said about the church, no clear definition has been given or established. Some like to define the church in terms of universal and local or invisible and visible, but these can be misunderstood and often misleading. Professor John Murray explains the following:

> According to the Scriptures we should speak of 'the church' and conceive of it as the *visible* entity that exists and functions in accord with the institution of Christ as its Head, the church that is the body of Christ and directed by the Holy Spirit, consisting of those sanctified in Christ Jesus and called to be saints, manifested in the congregations of the faithful. . .[5]

He further describes the church:

> [as] . . . the assembly of the covenant people of God, the congregation of believers, the household of God, the fellowship of the Holy Spirit, the body of Christ. It consists of men and women called by God the Father into the fellowship of His Son, sanctified in Christ Jesus, regenerated by His Spirit, and unified in the faith and confession of Christ Jesus as Lord and Saviour. Where there is such a communion gathered in Jesus' name, there is the church of God.[6]

Finally, he adds the following:

> It is important to bear in mind that the church of God is an institution. It may never be conceived of apart from the organization of the people of God in visible expression and in discharge of the ordinances instituted by Christ.[7]

---

[5] *Collected Writings of John Murray*, vol. 1 (Edinburgh: The Banner of Truth Trust, 1976), p. 236.

[6] Ibid., pp. 237-238.

[7] Ibid., pp. 238.

What, then, is the church? While there is a body universal, consisting of those who believe in Christ throughout all the ages, **the church is primarily a visible organization of baptized believers who assemble together to worship God and to obey Christ's commands.** Paul described it as being the "house of God, the pillar and ground of truth" (1 Timothy 3:15). Edward Hiscox gives an excellent summary definition:

> A Church is a company of disciples, baptized on a profession of their faith in Christ, united in covenant to maintain the ordinances of the Gospel, and the public worship of God; to live godly lives, and to spread abroad the knowledge of Christ as the Saviour of men.[8]

As we examine 1 Timothy 3:14-15, several features appear that give us a more exact definition. The context is that of Paul's giving qualifications for the offices of bishop and deacon (vv. 1-13). Realizing he may be delayed in coming to the young pastor, the apostle wants him to know that there are certain expectations of behavior required, not in the world, school, marketplace, or workplace, but in the visible church. He then gives **three** magnificent descriptions of the church.

The **first** description of the visible church is the *"house of God."*[9] How is it "God's house"? Not only because God is its architect, builder, owner, and provider, but because He dwells there. In the Old Testament, the first usage of the phrase *"house of God"* is in Genesis 28:16-17, where Jacob dreamed of a ladder *"set up on earth, and its top reached into heaven."* When Jacob woke up, he knew God was in that place and named it Bethel (Heb. – *house of God*). God continued to visibly manifest His presence to Israel

---

[8] *New Directory for Baptist Churches,* (American Baptist Publication Society, Philadelphia, PA, 1894), p. 15.

[9] *oiāko theou.*

by dwelling within the Tabernacle and, later, in the Temple built by Solomon (2 Chronicles 7:1-3). However, it must be remembered, that God is not limited to these places, which were subject to decay and destruction. He is present everywhere in the totality of His being, filling heaven and earth (1 Kings 8:27; Jeremiah 23:24). Even so, the infinite God, whom the heaven of heavens cannot contain, dwelt among His people. He is said to have had His tabernacle in Salem and to have dwelt in Zion (Psalm 76:2). He is even said to have dwelt between the cherubim, referring to the Ark of the Covenant (Psalm 80:1; cf. Exodus 25:22).

Thus, the title *"house of God"* emphasizes the place where God dwells. We must realize that the visible church is not simply a voluntary association of believers, but the very dwelling place of the triune God. As John Calvin states, "There are good reasons why God bestows this name on His Church; for not only has He received us to be His children by the grace of adoption, but He also dwells in the midst of us."[10]

In the New Covenant, God manifests His presence in His elect, redeemed, believing people, for each believer serves as the temple of God (1 Corinthians 3:16-17 & 6:19-20). However, when Paul speaks here of the *"house of God,"* he is not referring to the individual believer. Neither is he speaking of the universal body of believers, scattered throughout the world, but of the corporate body of believing members of a visible church. It is not in our individuality as believers that we are the "house of God," but in our corporateness as the gathered assembly. John R. W. Stott excellently captures the meaning of this description when he makes the following statement:

---

[10] *Sermons on Timothy and Titus* (Edinburgh: The Banner of Truth Trust, 1983), p. 88.

When the members of the congregation are scattered during most of the week it is difficult to remain aware of this reality [that God dwells among us]. But when we come together as *the church . . . of the living God,* every aspect of our common life is enriched by the knowledge of his presence in our midst. In our worship we bow down before the living God. Through the reading and exposition of his Word we hear his voice addressing us. We meet him at his table, when he makes himself known to us through the breaking of bread.[11]

This is what Paul means when he says that a well-ordered worship service in a church will cause the unbeliever who comes among us to sense the presence of God, fall down on his face, and report that *"truly God is among you"* (1 Corinthians 14:25). It is ". . . in the Church [that] God is pleased to manifest all the greatness of his love, all the marvelous depth of his compassion, and show himself to his people as he never did to the angels, and as he will never do to the unregenerate."[12]

The **second** description of the visible church is the *"church of the living God."*[13] *Ekklésia,* translated church, or a called-out assembly, is used five different ways in the NT Scriptures: 1) It is secular assembly (Acts 19:32, 39 & 41); 2) Stephen refers to Israel in her wilderness wanderings as a church (Acts 7:38); 3) It is the universal body of God's elect from the descent of the Holy Spirit at Pentecost to the second advent of Christ (Ephesians 1:22-23); 4) It is the final, culminated group of the redeemed, which is the church of the Firstborn, assembled in heaven (Hebrews 12:23); 5) It is the visible assembly of baptized believers, meeting in a specific location, organized under the

---

[11] *Guard The Truth* (Downers Grove: InterVarsity Press, 1996), p. 104.
[12] C.H. Spurgeon, *Metropolitan Tabernacle Pulpit,* vol. 54 (Pasadena, TX: Pilgrim Publications, 1978) p. 244.
[13] *ekklesia theou zontos.*

government of pastors and deacons, to perpetuate the ordinances of baptism and the Lord's Supper, and to propagate the gospel to the ends of the earth (Mark 16:15).

With this description, Paul emphasizes the aspect of being the "called out ones." It is God who is specifically calling sinners out of the world into His church and kingdom. As the living God, He is the church's builder by the effectual and almighty call of the gospel. According to Robert Gromacki, "In contrast to the Ephesian temples dedicated to nonexistent deities, living believers have been called out of the world of lost humanity by the one and only living God."[14]

Not only is Christ's church (manifested in visible congregations) in contrast to dead temples of nonexistent deities, but it is contrary to man-made, manipulative means often employed today to produce converts. Thus, Paul is saying that the church is God's building. It is a visible, living assembly built by the power of the living God. It is *His people*—sustained, nourished, and maintained by the power divine of Him who never dies, the true and living God. He ultimately oversees and preserves it unto His heavenly kingdom.

The **third** description of the visible church is the *"pillar and ground of truth."*[15] Truth is paramount. It is truth that will set us free from sin (John 8:32). It is truth that will lead us to Christ. It is truth that will save us. It is truth that will deliver us from error and keep our feet from falling. Contrary to Roman Catholicism, it is truth that gave life to the church, not vice versa. The church did not create redemptive truth. Actually, the truth, centered upon Christ's person and work and

---

[14] *Stand True To The Charge* (Grand Rapids: Baker Book House, 1982), p. 98.

[15] *stulos kaì edraiiama tes aletheias.*

revealed in the Old Testament Scriptures, gave birth to the NT church. The church, as God's dwelling place and building, has been given a commission. It is to be the pillar and ground (or foundation) of truth.

> No ordinary enhancement is derived from this appellation. Could it be described in loftier language? Is anything more venerable, or more holy, than that everlasting truth which embraces both the glory of God and the salvation of men? Were all the praises of heathen philosophy, with all it has been adorned by its followers, collected into one heap, what is this in comparison of the dignity of this wisdom, which alone deserves to be called light and truth, and the instruction of life, and the way, and the kingdom of God? Now it is preserved on earth by the ministry of the church alone.[16]

A pillar is to support and hold up the truth so that it can be seen of men. The ground is to be the foundation and mainstay upon which truth stands. Thus, the visible church has a unique commission. It *alone* is to support the truth, steady and firm, against the storms of heresy and unbelief. The church is to be a firm foundation against the propagators of error and falsehood. It must be solid so that truth does not collapse under the weight of false teaching. The church, with power divine, must maintain the truth at all costs. It *alone* is to elevate the truth in the defense and confirmation of the gospel. It is to hold truth high in the proclamation of the gospel. The church is not to advertise itself, but to advertise and display the unadulterated truth. Every member of the body, the church, must actively engage himself or herself in this two-fold duty.

Finally, it must be noted that the truth is not found in dreams, visions, fresh revelations, or in psychological meanderings of motivational sermons. Rather, it is found in the inspired,

---

[16] Calvin, *Sermons on Timothy and Titus,* p. 90.

inerrant, authoritative, infallible, clear, preserved, and sufficient Word of God—the Holy Scriptures. The Word is put forth by declaration: "*So then faith comes by hearing, and hearing by the Word of God*," (Romans 10:17). There can be no faith unless there is the proclamation of the Word of God and the gospel, and the visible church is the foundation from which these go forth.

These magnificent descriptions of the church confirm the primary definition of the church. *It is a visible body of believers, called out of the world by the living God Himself, gathered in holy covenant unto Him, with Him dwelling in their midst, upholding the truth, and being the foundation from which the Word and gospel go forth.*

DISCUSSION FOR CHAPTER THREE:

1. What are some confusing ideas about the nature and identity of the church?

2. List the reasons why the church needs repairing.

3. What is the main point of Professor John Murray's three quotes?

4. Discuss Hiscox's summary definition of the church.

5. What is the context of 1 Timothy 3:14-15?

6. Discuss the three descriptions of the church as found in 1 Timothy 3:14-15. How do they apply to you as a Christian?

4

THE CENTRALITY OF THE CHURCH
IN REDEMPTIVE HISTORY

*"To Him be glory in the church by Christ Jesus unto all generations,
world without end. Amen"*
(Ephesians 3:21)

WHAT DO WE UNDERSTAND by the term *redemptive history?* Since the Fall of mankind into sin in the Garden of Eden and the great promise of a Redeemer's coming forth from the *"seed of the woman"* to *"bruise the heel of the serpent"* (Genesis 3:15), God has been at work in the world, actively involved in redemption (i.e., rescuing and releasing people from sin and bringing them into fellowship with Himself). As the old saying goes, "History is *His* story." This is especially evident in the great redemptive acts throughout history.

In the course of the long and storied annals of time, the triune God has worked and operated through covenants. From the Covenant of Works with Adam, and the first manifestation of the Covenant of Grace in Eden (Genesis 3:15 & 21), to the culmination and fullness of all God's redemptive dealings with humanity in the New Covenant (see Jeremiah 31:29-34; cf. Hebrews 8:7-13), the LORD has been calling out a special people for Himself. The writer of Hebrews makes it clear that this New

Covenant, which has its origins in the "everlasting covenant," has Christ as its blood-shedding Mediator (Hebrews 13:20-21) for all who believe.[17] In this era of the New Covenant, the visible church is the central agent God uses to carry out all His redemptive purposes.

The church is the context in which God acts in the world. Paul the Apostle says, *"Unto Him be glory in the church by Christ Jesus unto all generations, world without end. Amen."* This verse is a doxology (a formula of praise to God), and it reveals Paul's focus of the Christian life and ministry. His entire being revolved around Christ and His visible churches. He did not dare think of Christ without thinking of the church. Paul was sent out on his first missionary journey from the church at Antioch (Acts13:1-4). Everywhere he went he preached the gospel, made converts, and established churches (Acts14:23). When Paul finished his missionary journey, he reported back to the sending church (Acts 14:26-28). He comprehended, along with John the Apostle, that when churches gather to worship God in spirit and in truth, the risen Lord Christ is in their midst. The Savior still walks among His lampstands!

Salvation and sanctification, as defined in the NT Scriptures, require the visible church. The ministry of the Word of God and the gospel, as found in the church, produce saving faith. The church's preaching of the "whole counsel of God" produces gospel holiness, sanctification, and growth in grace.

---

[17] Space and the intent of this book will not allow for a full treatment of God's divine covenants. For further study on this subject, see Louis Berkhof, *Systematic Theology New Combined Edition* (Grand Rapids: Wm. B. Eerdmans Publishing Co., 1996), pp. 262-301; Wayne Grudem, *Systematic Theology* (Grand Rapids: Zondervan, 2000), pp. 515-525; A.W. Pink, *The Divine Covenants* (Grand Rapids: Baker Book House) 1975. Also, see the author's booklet *Covenant Theology: A Reformed Baptist Overview* published by Reformed Baptist Publications; Carlisle, PA.

Someone has said, "Attempts to grow in Christ outside the church is like trying to swim without ever getting into the pool."[18] The church and its God-ordained leaders serve as a bulwark to guard believers from going astray and falling into apostasy. Godly pastors and elders are there as counselors and friends when believers enter hard times and difficulties. Being a member of a church will give Christians the love and service of fellow members. Brothers and sisters in Christ will be there to weep when one weeps, rejoice when one rejoices, and walk side by side with one another in the Christian life. *Paul knew to think lightly of the church is to think lightly of Christ.* How contrary is the thinking of many Christians today!

Ephesians 3:21 is a crucial verse to understanding Paul's mindset. In this verse Paul teaches *six* important facts about the church:

First, in all it does, the church is to be *God-centered* (*"unto Him"*). What is the Holy Bible all about? It is not primarily about science, medicine, history, economics, music, social order, jurisprudence, marriage and family, civil government, or a host of other subjects, though the Bible speaks with authority and infallibility on each of these subjects and more. The Holy Bible is primarily about one subject—God. A mega-clue is given for us in the very first verse of the *Holy Bible*: Genesis 1:1—*"In the beginning God. . ."* Thus, the church, as the people of God, is to be centered upon *"Him,"* in all His being, essence, nature, and attributes.

Second, the church is to be *purpose-centered* (*"be glory"*). In other words, the church's main purpose is to exist for God's glory.

---

[18] Wayne Mack & David Swavely, *Life in the Father's House* (Phillipsburg: Presbyterian & Reformed Publishing:, 1996), p. 13.

The glory of God is central to Himself and it is central to the church's existence. Everything God does is ultimately for His own glory; likewise, everything the church does should be for God's glory.

Third, the church is to be *organization-centered* (*"in the church"*). In other words, the church is a visible, structured body with a regenerate, recognizable membership that carries out its responsibilities with a constitution and order. We know that numerical records were kept from Pentecost forward (Acts 2:41, 4:4).

Fourth, the church is to be *Christ-centered* (*"by Christ Jesus"*). Christ, as revealed in the Scriptures, is the full and final manifestation of God. Therefore, the church is to feature every facet of His person and to focus on every aspect of His work.

Fifth, the church is to be *generation-centered* (*"through all ages"* or, literally, *"through all generations"*). The church is to minister and declare God's truth to every succeeding generation. The church must *not* yield to the present generation or be manipulated by its cultural whims and fancies. Each generation *must* yield to the truth of God as revealed in Word of God and proclaimed by the church. Generations change, but God's truth does not! Beware of the person who says truth changes.

Sixth, the church is to be *eternity-centered* (*"world without end"* or, literally, *"from the age to the ages"*). God has put eternity into the hearts of His people, and the church lives out its life with eternity in view. Central to all of God's redemptive purposes in Christ Jesus and the primary instrument for accomplishing them in the earth is the church.

DISCUSSION FOR CHAPTER FOUR:

1. What is meant by the phrase *redemptive history?*

2. What is the role of the church with regard to redemptive history?

3. How did Paul the Apostle's life and ministry revolve around visible churches?

4. List the benefits of the church to Christians and examine each one as it pertains to you personally.

5. Discuss the *six* important facts about the church found in Ephesians 3:21.

5

WHAT ARE THE MARKS OF A TRUE CHURCH?

"And if he refuses to hear them, tell it to the church.
But if he refuses even to hear the church,
let him be to you like a heathen and a tax collector."
(Matthew 18:17)

HISTORICALLY, THE CHURCH has been defined by certain "marks," or irreducible, non-negotiable elements. The Roman Catholic institution has defined itself as *the* Christian church characterized by an episcopal hierarchy, with the pope as its head, holding belief in saving sacraments and the authority of tradition, and being distinctly *one, holy, catholic* and *apostolic.* The Novations (3rd century) differed from the *catholic* and orthodox position over the re-admittance into the church of penitents who offered incense to Caesar during times of persecution. To them, the church should be marked as distinctly *pure.* The Donatists (4th and 5th centuries) continued the ideal of purity to further mark the church as distinctly *separated.* Through the centuries, others have wrestled exegetically with the Scriptures to discover the indispensable marks of a true church. Yet, very few have totally agreed with one another.

In the sixteenth century, heroic men, known as the Protestant Reformers, emerged out of the darkness of Medieval Europe, breaking the tyrannical and damnable stranglehold of Rome

33

over the common people. Through their efforts, light came over Western civilization with the realization of *"Post Tenebras Lux."*[19] They sought a return to the primitive church of the apostles. There is some discussion whether the Reformers believed there are two or three marks of a true church. It is generally held that they affirmed *three* indispensable marks of a true church.

The *first* mark of a true church, as held by the Reformers, was the true preaching of the Word through the practice of a thorough exposition of the Holy Scriptures. By this practice they asserted that everything in the church and life is subservient to the Word of God *alone*.[20] They held that tradition, though at times valuable, had no authority over the church. They translated the Word of God into the common languages of their day so that the average man, woman, and child could be well-versed in what God said. Thus, they expounded and preached through entire books of the Bible, chapter by chapter and verse by verse. Why did they do this? They understood the Holy Bible was the very Word of God and not the word of men (1 Thessalonians 2:13). Also, because God had *"manifested His Word through preaching"* (Titus 1:3), they believed that "the preaching of the Word of God *is* the Word of God (*emphasis added*)."[21] Calvin's *Commentaries* (twenty-two volumes), along with his printed sermons, are classic examples of this expression. The Reformers' famous war cry was *"Sola Scriptura."* The sixty-six books of the *Holy Bible* trumped the ensnaring, human traditions of the dark Medieval church. The Word was what the people of God needed most. Therefore, if a church did

---

[19] Latin, *after darkness light*. This expression is carved on granite in giant letters along the back wall of Calvin's Cathedral (St. Pierre's) in Geneva, Switzerland.

[20] Latin, *Sola Sriptura*.

[21] Latin, *Praedicatio Verbi Dei Verbum Dei est*. Taken from Bullinger's *Confessio Helvetica Posterior*.

not provide a thorough exposition of the Word of God, it was not deemed a true church.

The *second* mark of a true church, according to the Reformers, was a proper view and observance of the sacraments.[22] A study of the NT and early Christian history shows that the apostolic and post-apostolic churches had *only* two ordinances: baptism and the Lord's Supper. Baptism, upon a credible confession of faith, is a recognized mark of entrance into the covenant community of the church. Edmund Clowney correctly asserts, "Baptism administered apart from any creditable profession of faith on the part of those claiming God's promise ceases to function as a mark of the church."[23] In the *"breaking of bread,"* or partaking of the Lord's Table, the church testifies of her ongoing communion and fellowship with the ascended Christ, as they remember Him and proclaim *"the Lord's death until He comes"* (1 Corinthians 11:26). The Reformers correctly understood that the sacraments were not saving, but outward, visible signs of inward, invisible grace. Without these Christ-ordained symbols, a church was not a true church.

As the early churches grew more formal and works-oriented, other man-made practices were added to the list of ordinances. Traveling through the centuries and arriving at the present, we find Roman Catholicism has seven *saving* sacraments—Baptism, Confirmation, Holy Communion, Confession, Marriage, Holy Orders, and the Anointing of the Sick (known as "extreme unction" when performed upon the dying).

---

[22] Latin, *sacramentum*, meaning *a thing sacred*. I am not opposed to using the word *sacrament*, if it is properly understood as sacred, instead of saving. Historically, and more often than not, Baptists have preferred the word *ordinance*, meaning *something ordained* (e.g., Christ ordained/established baptism and the Lord's Supper).
[23] *The Church*, (Downers Grove: InterVarsity Press, 1996) p. 105.

The Reformers studied the Scriptures and soundly rejected these seven due to their lack of biblical and exegetical foundation. They realized that in the Roman institution ". . . impiety so stalked abroad, that almost no doctrine of religion was pure from admixture, no ceremony free from error, no part . . . of divine worship untarnished by superstition."[24] Superstition abounded and the sacraments had been "adulterated," to use Calvin's strong word.[25] Rather than revamping the manufactured, traditional seven, the Reformers returned to the inspired, apostolic two (baptism and the Lord's Supper). They further established that these must be performed within the realm of the church and administered only by those appointed from within the church. If the ordinances were administered outside the boundaries of the church, by anyone who took it upon himself to do such, the ordinances were considered invalid.

The *third* mark of a true church, according to the Reformers, was a careful and faithful exercising of church discipline. If the Word and sacraments (i.e., ordinances) were the entrance into the church, church discipline was necessary to maintain the identity of those who entered. The church, being called out of the world, could not think, live, or act like the world. If love and devotion to Christ did not constrain church members to live holy and Christlike lives and they fell into public and scandalous sins, then a faithful and careful discipline was to be exercised. Discipline was necessary to maintain the testimony of Christ before the eyes of a watching world and to prevent Christ from coming against His church "with the sword of . . . [His] mouth" (Revelation 2:12 & 16).[26] These were not the

---

[24] John Calvin, "Reply to Sadoleto," *Tracts and Treatises*, vol. I, (Grand Rapids: Wm. B. Eerdmans Publishing Co. 1948) p. 49.

[25] Ibid., p. 49.

[26] *The Westminster Confession of Faith* describes this as "the wrath of God, which might justly fall upon the church," (30: III).

only purposes of church discipline, however. There was another goal: the full recovery and restoration of the sinning believer. They were careful to distinguish between formative discipline, which continually took place under the ministry of the Word, and censorial discipline (censures), which occurred for lesser offenses that only affected the body, and excommunication, which removed a sinning member who refused to repent of flagrant, public sin. Excommunication was the last step, not the first, in the disciplinary process. If there existed no exercise of biblical discipline in the church, the church ceased to be a true church.

Theodore Beza summarizes the Protestant Reformers' view of the marks of a true church when he asserts the following:

> To conclude, in what place the Word of God is purely preached, the Sacraments purely administered, and ecclesiastical discipline conducted conformably to the holy and pure doctrine, there we recognize the Church of God, no matter how few (Matt. 18:20; Luke 12:32) or small of appearance in men's eyes (Luke 10:21; I Cor. 1:19-28; Matt. 11:17).[27]

Today, there are pastor-scholars who, studying the picture of the first church in Acts 2:40-42, have concluded that there are four basic marks of a true New Testament church. They are the apostle's doctrine, fellowship, breaking of bread (Communion), and prayers.[28] Some, however, have concluded that these "four" leave gaps. Mark Dever has expanded the topic and written an excellent book, entitled *Nine Marks of a Healthy Church.*[29]

---

[27] *The Christian Faith* (East Sussex: Focus Christian Ministries Trust, 1992) p. 73.

[28] e.g., John MacArthur, pastor-teacher of Grace Community Church in Sun Valley, California.

[29] Wheaton: Crossway Books, 2004. By his own admission, Dr. Dever's book is not "an exhaustive ecclesiology" (p. 16). All of his nine marks revolve around two basic needs of churches: "the preaching of the message and the leading of disciples" (p. 28).

What, then, are the marks of a true church of Jesus Christ? The following are *five* irreducible, non-negotiable attributes that constitute an ideal local church (see Acts 2:41-47; et al):

First, a true church is a visible body that is continually under the government and rule of the Holy Scriptures, the Word of God. This is demonstrated by thorough expository preaching and teaching of the whole counsel of God (i.e., *"the apostles' doctrine"*), line upon line and precept upon precept. The pulpit, not an altar, will be central in the church building.

Second, a true church is a visible body led and directed by scripturally-qualified men, who are under the authority of Christ the Head and answerable only to Him and the congregation. The only officers in a NT church are pastors and deacons.[30] No entity or person, outside of each visible church, has authority over the church. These men *must* meet the qualifications listed in 1 Timothy 3:1-7 (cf. Titus 1:5-9), if they are to be pastors, and listed in 1 Timothy 3:8-13, if they are to be deacons. Giftedness is not the first or chief prerequisite for the pastoral or diaconal ministry. Of the nineteen qualifications for a pastor (bishop, elder) and ten qualifications for a deacon, only one deals with giftedness—*"able to teach."* It is imperative that grace and godliness characterize the one called into office.

Third, a true church is a visible body who faithfully, reverently, and joyfully observes the only two ordinances of the gospel—baptism and the Lord's Supper. Members understand their scripturalness and sacredness. The ordinances are observed on a

---

[30] Contrary to modern baptistic beliefs, deacons do not rule or lead in Christ's churches. They are called to serve the physical needs of the church (with grace), and are under the authority of the pastors/elders. The authority deacons possess is not their own, but a delegated authority received from the pastors, who receive theirs from Christ and His Word.

consistent basis and are not simply "tacked on" to the end of a worship service.

Fourth, a true church is a visible body that compassionately exercises church discipline. While no Christian is perfect or has achieved perfection, the process of sanctification demands that the believer strive for Christlikeness and holiness. The follower of Christ bears the name of Christ and carries the testimony of Christ in his or her work-a-day world; therefore, he or she must seek to live a life commensurate with that name and testimony. If correction becomes necessary, the Holy Bible prescribes a disciplinary process. Initially, the misconduct must be addressed by individual members (1 Thessalonians 5:14-15, cf. Matthew 18:15), then by the pastors and elders if early attempts do not succeed, and, finally, by the body corporate if there is no genuine repentance (Matthew 18:16-20; 1 Corinthians 5:1-13, esp. vv. 4-5). Love for Christ and one's fellow member demands compassionate church discipline. One of the most *unloving* things a church can do to one of its members is to not exercise church discipline, when needed.

Fifth, a true church is a visible body that has a vibrant Christian life. Vibrancy in the church is evidenced in several ways:

• There is spiritual worship, contrary to starched, stifling deadness on the one hand and an unbridled, emotional frenzy on the other. Christ taught that the Father seeks people to worship Him *"in spirit and in truth"* (John 4:24). Spiritual worship engages all of the ransomed powers of the believer.[31]

---

[31] Some have taken "spirit" in this verse to mean the Holy Spirit. However, I believe due to the lack of the definite article and the qualifying adjective "holy" before or after the word "spirit," it refers to the human spirit. Christ is teaching that worship must *not* be in sterile truth and outward forms only, but from the

- There is fellowship and brotherly love. The members genuinely care for each other, regardless of status in society, level of education, or cultural background. Christians rejoice with those who rejoice and weep with those who weep (Romans 12:15).

- Since believers have been predestinated to be conformed to the image of Christ (Romans 8:29), there will be a degree of sanctification and holiness of life in each. As it was with ancient Israel, so it is with the church today: God has made a difference between His people and the world (1 Corinthians 4:7; 2 Corinthians 5:17; cf. Exodus 11:7). This difference must be exhibited in a heart and manner of living, contrary to the heart and lifestyle of the world.

- There will be meetings of corporate prayer, in which the congregation brings its petitions, intercessions, and supplications before the throne of grace (Hebrews 4:14-16). These meetings will not be Bible studies with a couple of people praying at the end. Instead, they will be specifically set-aside times during which the entire body collectively beseeches the triune God of heaven to work, act, move, bless, and do impossible things that cannot be attributed to human workings. Not only should there be much prayer, but fervent prayer, warm prayer, and expectant prayer. Why pray if you do not expect God the LORD to answer and bless? If a church does not have corporate meetings for prayer, it cannot claim to be biblical and apostolic (Act 2:41d; 1 Timothy 2:1 ff.).

---

entire inner being of the regenerate. It is easy to sit in a service of worship and go through the forms and motions without ever engaging the mind, soul, spirit, heart, emotions, and will. This must not be!

- There will be evangelism and missions. The last words of Christ, before ascending into heaven, are what is called the Great Commission (Matthew 28:18-20; Mark 16:15-16; Luke 24:46-48; John 20:21; Acts 1:8). The visible church is responsible for fulfilling what was initially delegated to the apostles. There will be corporate efforts to ensure that the gospel is proclaimed in neighborhoods, cities, states, and taken to the ends of the earth. Furthermore, a vibrant church will contain individuals who desire to tell others *"what great things Christ has done"* for them and how He has had *"compassion"* on them (Luke 8:39; Mark 5:19).

- There will be works of charity and benevolence towards those inside and outside the church. Genuine needs will be met, as the church has ability and opportunity. This does not mean the church indiscriminately gives away money, food, and clothes. Instead, the key to understanding such passages as Acts 2:44-45 and 4:34-35 lies in the little expression *"as anyone had need."* Where there is legitimate need, the church will dig deep into its treasury and demonstrate its charity by giving benevolently.

These are the marks and attributes, irreducible and non-negotiable, which set aside a visible church of Jesus Christ from all other organizations in the world. Without these marks, a church ceases to be a true church.

DISCUSSION FOR CHAPTER FIVE:

1. How did/does the historical Roman Catholic institution define itself?

2. What are the three marks of a true church, as held by the Protestant Reformers of the 16th century?

3. According to Acts 2:40-42, what do some modern pastor-scholars teach are the four marks of a true church?

4. Discuss what essentials you think have been largely lost in today's churches.

5. What are the *five* irreducible, non-negotiable marks that constitute an ideal visible church?

6. How is vibrancy shown and seen in local church life?

6

WHAT IS THE PURPOSE OF THE CHURCH?

"Whether therefore you eat or drink, or whatsoever you do,
do all to the glory of God."
(1 Corinthians 10:31)

THE EXISTENCE AND NATURE of the church cannot be separated from its purpose. Today, many believe the primary purposes of the church are to feed the poor, to educate the illiterate, to teach the underprivileged and underdeveloped nations how to farm, build homes, and establish welfare systems, and to promote liberation from tyrannical governments. This is called the "social gospel." While there is a legitimate need for many of these activities in the world today, these are not the church's primary responsibilities. The "social gospel" is not the gospel at all; it can be used as a subtle device of Satan to sidetrack true churches of God from their main purpose.

The church has one overarching, main purpose: to glorify God (1 Corinthians 10:31; Ephesians 3:21). Every aspect of the church's life should be carried out with that goal in mind. While there are many ways a church can glorify God, we shall consider *three* elements, which are simple but all inclusive.

Biblical worship is the *first* element in the purpose of the church to glorify God (Ephesians 1:3-14, 3:21; 1 Peter 4:10-11). The individual Christian is to come together with other Christians and in a corporate manner to worship the triune God. A true church of Jesus Christ is first a worshipping body. The Lord Jesus promised that where two or three are gathered in His name, there He will be in their midst (Matthew 18:20). In the Gospel of John, as Jesus spoke to the woman at the well, He proclaimed that the Father is seeking people who will worship Him in spirit and truth (John 4:24). If God is seeking people to worship Him in this way, then corporate adoration should be regular, active, and fervent on the part of the visible church.

Corporate worship consists of reading the Scriptures, prayer, praise (psalms, hymns and spiritual songs), thanksgiving, giving of tithes and offerings, and observing the ordinances of the gospel. The most important aspect of worship, however, is the proclamation of the Word of God through expository preaching. To neglect collective worship with believers is to break God's command and sin against Him (Hebrews 10:25).[32]

Instruction and edification of believers is the *second* element in the purpose of the church to glorify God. This is what Christ meant when He said "*. . . teaching them to observe all things that I have commanded you. . .*" (Matthew 28:20; cf. 1 Thessalonians 5:11-13). The Lord's people are often destroyed because they lack knowledge. Instruction in the Word of God, by men who are "*apt to teach,*" is necessary for the Christian if he is to stand in this evil world. God has ordained it to be this way. Those who are saved need to be instructed line upon line, precept upon

---

[32] Some do not believe that Hebrews 10:25 applies to the visible church. This idea will be discussed later.

precept, expositorily through the Bible. A light textual sermon, a casual skimming of Scripture passages, or a motivational "pep talk," with a few verses of the Bible thrown in here and there, will not suffice.

As the Christian is properly instructed and taught the Word of God, he is edified and the building-up process takes place. Paul the Apostle says that Christ, upon His ascension into heaven, *"gave gifts of . . . pastors and teachers; for the equipping of the saints for the work of ministry, for the **edifying** of the body of Christ. . ."* (Ephesians 4:11-16). The Greek word from which we get "edify" actually means "to build a house."[33] The English word "edifice," which means a building, comes from this same word. Just as a blacksmith cannot forge horseshoes without an anvil, neither can a Christian be built up in the faith and established in grace without the ministry of instruction and edification that is found in the visible church and directed by men called of God.

Churches today, in general, are in an anemic state and believers are languishing as never before. They hardly know what or why they believe, if they believe anything at all. This is because men who profess themselves to be preachers and ministers have *not* been faithful to the God-appointed task of declaring the whole counsel of God. Many have become more proficient at telling jokes, giving personal experiences, recounting anecdotes, and using illustrations, rather than being adequate exegetes and declarers of the Word. The crying need of the hour is for faithful, consistent, and fervent expository preaching that will instruct and build up believers. May Christ give to His churches many great and faithful men who will carry out this noble task.

---

[33] *oikodomen.*

The *last* element in the purpose of the church to glorify God is the evangelization of the world with the gospel (Matthew 28:18-20; Mark 16:15; Luke 24:46-48). While many put great emphasis upon evangelism, very little true evangelism is taking place. Biblical evangelism is defined by Ernest Reisinger as follows:

> To present Jesus Christ to sinful men, in order that they may come to put their trust in God . . . to receive Him [Christ] as their Saviour and serve Him as their King in the fellowship of the church. You will notice that this definition is more than 'winning souls' or saving people from hell, or saving them from their personal problems, or from life's casualties and you will notice that the definition includes serving Christ in His Church.[34]

Mr. Reisinger then adds, "Much present-day evangelism would not fit this definition."

Before the Christian will zealously and freely witness to the lost, he or she must worship the great triune God. After worshipping the LORD God of heaven and earth, by the Holy Spirit, and being built up (edified) in their faith, the believer will then go forth with words of reconciliation upon his or her lips and tell this world doomed in darkness and sin about the Savior of sinners.

Thus, the three major elements through which the visible church is to glorify God are biblical worship, instruction and edification of believers, and evangelization of the world with the gospel of Christ. These three must be *equally* present in a visible church for the people of God to be balanced, fully developed, and vigorous in their Christian lives.

---

[34] *Today's Evangelism* (Phillipsburg: Craig Press, 1982) p. 1-2. Pastor Reisinger is partially quoting from J. I. Packer, *Evangelism and the Sovereignty of God.*

DISCUSSION FOR CHAPTER SIX:

1. What are some false notions about the church's purpose often held by the secular world?

2. What is the one true purpose of a church?

3. What are the three elements in which a church can carry out its one true purpose? Discuss each one.

4. Why must these three elements be *equally* present in a church?

7

IS MEMBERSHIP IN A CHURCH BIBLICAL?

"Yet none of the rest dared join them, but the people esteemed them highly.
And believers were increasingly added to the Lord,
multitudes of both men and women."
(Acts 5:13-14)

MANY CHRISTIANS STRONGLY oppose church membership because the phrase "church membership" is not found in the Bible. Although the phrase is not mentioned, the teaching and principle are obviously present and practiced. The NT assumes and takes for granted that a convert will be baptized, join a body of baptized believers, and submit to those who have the rule and oversight of each assembly (see Acts 2:41-47). It should be noted that the word "church" in verse 47 is not an invisible body of the faithful, but a *visible* body of baptized believers.

An examination of the NT reveals that certain passages prove that the early churches had a formal, official membership. These passages of Scripture deal with church issues and can be placed in *three* categories: church discipline, church leaders, and church benevolence.

The *first* category of Scripture, which deals with church membership, is in the area of church discipline. Matthew 18:15-

17, the second place in the NT where the word "church" is mentioned, deals with church discipline. In this passage, Christ gives the principle and order of what is to be done if a Christian trespasses or sins against another Christian. In the disciplinary process, if the first two steps (vv. 15-16) fail, the third step that must take place is outlined in verse 17: *"If he shall neglect to hear them [the two or three witnesses who confronted the sinning brother], tell it to the church. . ."* What is the "church" that is spoken of here? Is it a spiritual, mystical body, or is it a visible congregation? If it is the spiritual, mystical body of Christians scattered all over the world, it would be impossible to recognize them. The rest of verse 17 bears out the fact that the church is a visible congregation: *"but if he neglects to hear the church, let him be unto you as a heathen man and a publican."* There must have been some type of union and formal membership in order for the individual to be cast out and treated as a pagan and tax collector.

In Acts 5:1-11, we find the account of Ananias and Sapphira. After this deceitful couple had lied to God, the Holy Spirit, and the apostles, they suffered death by God's judgment. Verse 13 demonstrates that this assembly was a visible congregation (not a spiritual, universal body). Witnessing God's judgment poured out upon the erring, professing believers within the church, the unconverted were dissuaded from attempting to *"join"* the membership of the local church at Jerusalem. Outsiders were fearful to not only *"join,"* but to even identify with the assembly.[35]

---

[35] *kollasthai* – has the aspect of not just joining, but of even daring to approach. See also Acts 9:26, where the same word is used, when Barnabas brought Saul to Jerusalem. There Saul (later to become Paul) "tried to *join* the disciples," but was not allowed.

Another passage of Scripture concerning church discipline is 1 Corinthians 5. Paul writes to the church at Corinth because there was illicit sex among them. A man was committing incestual fornication with his stepmother. In verse 2, Paul rebukes the church because they are puffed up and have not mourned over this deed. Also, he observes that this sinful man has not been put out of their midst. He admonishes them in verse 4, saying that when they are gathered in the name of Christ, they are to deliver such a one over to Satan for the destruction of the flesh. In verses 6-8, he tells the Corinthians to purge the old leaven; in verses 9-11, he writes that they are not to keep company with fornicators. Paul does not have in mind fornicators in the world, who are lost, but fornicators who call themselves brethren. With these they were not even to share meals! Paul sums up the chapter, in verses 12 and 13: *"For what have I to do with judging those who are outside? Do you not judge those who are inside? But those who are outside God judges."* The key phrase of the entire chapter is, *"Therefore put away from yourselves that wicked person."* If there had not been a formal membership, how could they put people from out of their midst?

These three passages of Scripture, which deal with church discipline (Matthew 18:15-17; Acts 5:1-11; 1 Corinthians 5:1-13), obviously demonstrate that there was a formal and recognizable membership in the early NT churches.

The *second* category of Scripture which teaches that the early churches had a membership is in the area of church leaders. In this category there are also key passages. Acts 6:1-8 introduces us to one of the first internal church problems. Murmuring had arisen among the Grecian-Jewish believers because their widows were neglected in the daily ministration. In other words, their widows were not being properly cared for in the physical realms of food, clothing, and, possibly, shelter. (Ethnic/cultural bias was present, even in the early church.)

The apostles, knowing that it was not good for them to leave the Word of God and serve widows' tables, commanded, *"Therefore, brethren, seek out from among you seven men of good reputation, full of the Holy Spirit and wisdom, whom we may appoint over this business."* The saying pleased the whole multitude; therefore, they chose seven men *"from among themselves,"* who were members of the church at Jerusalem, to carry out the duties of what is now known as the diaconate. The first deacons, therefore, came from the confines of the membership of the visible church, not from men who had *not* covenanted themselves with that particular body. God's blessing and approval on this is seen in that, immediately, the Word of God began to spread and the number of disciples greatly multiplied.

Sections in the Pastoral Epistles which deal with church officers further illuminate the truth that the visible churches had a formal membership. The qualifications for pastors/elders (bishops) and deacons *are never divorced from the visible church context* (1 Timothy 3:1-15; Titus 1:4-9). Paul makes this clear, in verses 14 and 15 of 1 Timothy 3, when he describes the visible assembly as *"the house of God, which is the church of the living God, the pillar and ground of truth."* The inspired apostle teaches that there are only two offices in the church, those of pastor and deacon; before a man can be brought into either office, he must be known and examined by the visible church to see if he meets the qualifications given in Scripture. This is possible only if the man is a member of a particular congregation.

Furthermore, Paul reminds the young pastor Timothy not to neglect the gift that was conveyed on him at his ordination (i.e., *"the laying on of the hands of the presbytery"* – 1 Timothy 4:14). George W. Knight III notes that this phrase (*"the laying on of the hands"*) is only found four times in the NT and is called "an act of ordination," and "the presbytery"[36] is a word that refers "generally to a council or college of elders."[37] Ordination to office is not a spiritual function of the church universal, but a ministerial function of the church visible. The ministry of the Word is always connected with visible, local churches. *It must be noted that the NT does not sanction any ministry that is separate from a church!*

The General Epistles also address the responsibilities of visible church leaders and church members. Hebrews 13:7 and 17 speak about a two-fold work of pastors: the first being to *"rule over you"* (cf. 1 Timothy 3:4-5) and the second being to *"watch out for your souls."* (NOTE: Ruling and watching are done primarily through the public ministry of the Word.) The two-fold response of believers is to *"remember"* and to *"be submissive."* The questions must be asked, "In what dimension do these actions take place?" and "How can these be exercised if there is no organized church or formal church membership?"

Three more examples from the General Epistles regarding church leaders reinforce the reality of church membership. One example is found in James 5:14. In this passage direction is given for believers who are sick. What are they to do? The sick are to *"call for the elders of the church."* To which church is the Apostle James referring, the universal or visible? The answer is obvious. Similarly, the Apostle Peter exhorts *"the elders who are among you . . .* [to] *shepherd the flock of God"* (1 Peter 5:1-4). As

---

[36] *tou presbuteriou.*
[37] NIGTC, *The Pastoral Epistles* (Grand Rapids: Wm. B. Eerdmans Publishing Co., 1992), p. 209.

"overseers" they were not to lord it over *"those entrusted to"* them. What *"flock"* are they to *"shepherd"* and *"oversee,"* the universal or visible? Again, the answer is clear. Another example (this time with a bad leader) is found in 3 John 9-10. We are informed of a wicked, authoritarian *church* leader named Diotrephes, who was *"putting [brethren] out of the church"* (3 John 9-10). How could this wicked man put brethren out of the church universal? He could not! This statement could only be made with reference to a visible church.

All of these passages from the General Epistles clearly demonstrate that there were visible churches, with formal memberships, that were to be ruled by scripturally-qualified and church-recognized pastors (i.e., elders). Only someone willfully blind, who refuses to see, would argue against the visible church and official membership in one.

Scriptures containing the accounts of church leaders who were chosen as church messengers to bear letters to other churches are additional proofs of church membership (Acts 15:22-31, 18:27; 2 Corinthians 8:18-24). These messengers were approved and appointed by the churches to be their spokesmen and representatives. Only those who were known and had a good report *in the congregations* were so commissioned.

The *last* category of Scripture which deals with church membership is in the area of benevolence, particularly pertaining to the care of widows. First Timothy 5:9-16 describes one aspect of the social program of the early churches. Verse 9 reads, *"Let not a widow under sixty years old be taken into the number, and not unless she has been the wife of one man . . .".* What does this mean? This passage reveals that within the membership of the NT churches, there was a sub-membership. It was a special list or roll for widows. The widows that were *"widows indeed"* were to be cared for by local congregations. In order for a widow to be physically supported, she had to be a member in good standing in a specific church and she had to meet the requirements listed in verses 9 and 10. If she met the requirements, she was placed on the widows' roll and taken care of physically. Paul concluded that as long as the widow had living, believing relatives, she was to be taken care of by them and not by the church. This passage offers another positive testimony from Scripture and history of church membership in the NT.

DISCUSSION FOR CHAPTER SEVEN:

1. What is assumed and taken for granted in the New Testament?

2. What are the three categories of Scripture passages that prove the early church had a membership?

3. How are these categories beneficial to Christ's churches today?

4. If being a part of the universal body of believers *only* is all that matters, why did Paul give such extensive lists of qualifications for bishops and deacons (1 Timothy 3:1-7, cf. Titus 1:4-9; 1 Timothy 3:8-13)?

5. Who can be an elder or deacon? How important is it for one to meet the biblical qualifications of these offices?

6. What relevance can *"submit to them that have rule over you"* (Hebrews 13:7 & 13) have in your life, if you are not a member of a visible church?

7. How can pastors (elders) *"shepherd"* and *"oversee"* you (1 Peter 5:1-2), if you are not part of a *"flock"*?

8. How would it be possible for 1 Timothy 5:9 to be implemented if a widow were not a formal member of a church?

IS MEMBERSHIP IN A CHURCH ESSENTIAL?

"To the intent that now the manifold wisdom of God might be made known by the church to the principalities and powers in heavenly places..."
(Ephesians 3:10)

THIS CAN BE A DIFFICULT and somewhat misleading question. Is church membership essential for salvation? For being brought into saving union with the Lord Jesus Christ? For having one's sins forgiven? For entering into heaven at last? The answer to all of these questions is a resounding—No!

Church membership *is* essential, however, in two aspects of the Christian life. It is essential for the believer to grow in grace and obedience to the Word of God, and it is essential for the visible church itself. Before considering these two essential aspects of church membership, let us consider some objections that are raised against church membership.

The *first* objection is that the term "church membership" does not appear in the Scriptures. It is argued that Jesus does not (nor does any other NT writer) ever mention or expressly teach formal membership in a visible church. Therefore, the argument continues, to insist upon it is to add to the Word of God and thus require believers to obey man-made rules.

The reply is very simple. This is the fallacious *word-thing* argument, which states that the absence of a certain word or phrase indicates the absence of the particular truth. While the term "church membership" does not appear in the Scripture, the evidences of church membership are apparent. Consider the fact that the words "trinity" and "virgin birth" do not appear in the Scriptures. It would be fallacious to argue against the teaching of these terms because the doctrines of and evidences for both truths are very clear in the Bible. Such is the case with church membership.

The *second* objection is that church membership is legalistic. This attitude is summed up in the notion that membership is part of dead "church-anity," something that is a part of lifeless orthodoxy.

The answer to this objection is that membership is not legalistic because of the very meaning of legalism. Theologically, legalism is doing anything to merit or earn God's salvation and grace. Obedience to any precept or principle of Scripture is *not* legalism but, rather, love and gospel obedience. Church membership is neither set forth in the Scriptures nor sought after as a requirement for salvation; there is no explicit connection between membership and salvation.

The *third* objection is the argument that all believers are members of the universal body of Christ; therefore, membership in a visible assembly is unnecessary. Since all are equally blood-bought saints, and all have access by one sacrifice to God the Father, there is no need for identification with a visible church.

Again, the answer is obviously simple. Once more, review the third biblical evidence in Chapter 2 that the NT is a church book. In response to the objection, if the overwhelming thrust of the NT were that of the "universal" church, several questions could be asked. Where does this "universal" church assemble for worship? When does it meet for worship? Who are its officers? What are their qualifications for office? How are they chosen? How does it send out missionaries, as was done in Acts 13:1-4 and 14:26-27? Who handles the offerings (i.e., *"collections"*) that are to be laid aside *"on the first day of the week"* (1 Corinthians 16:1-2)?

While all regenerate souls in all ages are members of the blood-bought body of Christ, having free access to God the Father without the intermediacy of priest or clergy, the LORD God has called each believer in every age to join himself to a visible assembly/church. Evidence for this is seen in a contextual examination of the twenty-four *"one another"* passages in the NT:

- *"Be kindly affectionate to one another"* (Romans 12:10)
- *"Edify one another"* (Romans 14:19; 1 Thessalonians 5:11)
- *"Be likeminded to one another"* (Romans 15:5)
- *"Admonish one another"* (Romans 15:14)
- *"Have the same care for one another"* (1 Corinthians 12:25)
- *"By love serve one another"* (Galatians 5:13)
- *"Be kind to one another"* (Ephesians 4:32a)
- *"Forgiving one another"* (Ephesians 4:32b; Colossians 3:13b)
- *"Submitting yourselves to one another"* (Ephesians 5:21)
- *"Forbearing one another"* (Colossians 3:13a)
- *"Admonishing one another"* (Colossians 3:16)
- *"Abound in love toward one another"* (1 Thessalonians 3:12, 4:9)
- *"Comfort one another"* (1 Thessalonians 4:18)

- *"Exhort one another"* (Hebrews 3:13, 10:25)
- *"Consider one another"* (Hebrews 10:24)
- *"Confess your faults to one another"* (James 5:16a)
- *"Pray for one another"* (James 5:16b)
- *"Love one another with a pure heart"* (1 Peter 1:22)
- *"Use hospitality toward one another"* (1 Peter 4:9)
- *"Be subject to one another"* (1 Peter 5:5)

How could these injunctions find any viable application outside a local, visible body of Christ?

It is interesting to note what the early Baptist leaders thought of membership in a visible church:

> The catholic or universal church, which (with respect to the internal work of the Spirit and truth of grace) may be called invisible, consists of the whole number of the elect that have been, are, or shall be gathered into one, under Christ, the head thereof; and is the spouse, the body, the fullness of Him that fills all in all.

> All persons throughout the world, professing the faith of the gospel, and obedience unto God by Christ according unto it, not destroying their own profession by any errors everting the foundation, or unholiness of conversion, are and may be called visible saints; and of such ought all particular congregations to be constituted.

> In the execution of this power wherewith He is entrusted, the Lord Jesus calls out of the world unto Himself, through the ministry of the Word, by His Spirit, those that are given into Him by His Father, that they may walk before Him in all ways of obedience, which He prescribes to them in His Word. Those thus called, He commands to walk together in particular societies, or

churches, for their mutual edification, and the due performance of that public worship, which He requires of them in the world.[38]

Having looked at the objections to church membership, let us now consider the reasons that membership is essential. ***Church membership is essential for one who has God as his Father to grow in grace*** (2 Peter 3:18). Cyprian, an early church father, declared, "He cannot have God for his Father who does not have the Church for his Mother. . . " We have already covered the purpose of the church concerning edification. Yet, there is an added dimension that has to do with the believer's being considered as part of the people of God. Before his conversion, the believer was noticeably part of the people of the world and under Satan's dominion (John 8:44; Ephesians 2:1-3). At conversion, through repentance toward God and faith in the Lord Jesus Christ, the Christian has God as his Father and has become part of the observable people of God. The LORD'S people have their visible expression in the form of a local church, from which they derive their name. R.C. Sproul gives interesting insight into this connection:

> The title *Lord* functions so frequently in the life of the New Testament community that the word *church* derives from it. The Greek word for church is *ekklesia*, which is brought over into the English in the word *ecclesiastical*. The English word *church* is similar in sound and form to other languages' words for church. *Kirk* in Scotland, *kerk* in Holland, and *kirsche* in German all derive from the same root. That source is the Greek word *kuriache*, which means 'those who belong to the

---

[38] *The London Baptist Confession of Faith of 1689:* Chapter 26, paragraphs 1, 2, and 5. I have slightly modernized the spelling by capitalizing all pronouns referring to deity and removing and replacing the "eth" with the proper tense word.

kurios.' Thus the word church in its literal origin means, 'the people who belongs to the Lord.'[39]

Why did the LORD make believers in Christ His people? The answer is simple: He did it in order that they might have strength and help in their growth in grace, their pilgrimage toward heaven, and conformity to the likeness of Christ. No Christian was ever meant to be alone! Again, R.C. Sproul puts it quite well:

> We need the church as much as a starving baby needs his mother's milk. We cannot grow or be nourished without the church. Possessing Christ and despising the church is an intolerable contradiction which none can bear. We cannot have Christ without embracing the church.[40]

Growth in grace and conformity to Christ comes about, in part, by obeying the express command of God to meet together with other people of God. This is the clear meaning of Hebrews 10:25: *"not forsaking the assembling* (Gk. - *episunagoge*; lit. - upon synagogue) *of ourselves together, as is the manner of some, but exhorting one another, and so much the more as you see the Day approaching."* It is obvious that the one who denies this verse applies to the visible church does not understand the verse. If the writer simply meant getting together for informal fellowship, he would have used another word rather than *"episunagoge."* As the Christian meets with the brethren in the church, he is encouraged and stirred up to love and good works, which are part of growth and obedience. This cannot be accomplished if a believer does not submit himself to his brethren and covenant together with them in a visible body of Christ. Thus, church membership is essential for the believer to grow in the Christian life.

---

[39] *Who Is Jesus?* (Wheaton: Tyndale House Publishers, Inc., 1983) p. 35.
[40] Ibid., p. 14.

The second reason that church membership is essential is for the well-being of the visible church itself. There are several reasons for this statement, all of which seem foreign to the modern Christian mind. While many think of the needs of the individual, we must not forget the church's needs and her testimony of Christ before a watching world. Christ's visible churches, which are His representatives on earth, have certain needs if they are to preserve their existence and testimony. Let us consider how church membership is essential for the church itself.

Church membership is essential for the doctrinal integrity of the body. Often the expression is heard that "Doctrine divides, but Jesus unites." That cliché sounds good on the surface, but underneath it is filled with holes that weaken the very foundation of biblical Christianity. Doctrine (or teaching) has always been important to Christ and His people. Christ came teaching doctrine and people were astonished because He taught with authority (Matthew 7:28-29). The early church continued steadfastly in the apostles' doctrine (Acts 2:42). Paul the Apostle exhorted ministers to take heed to themselves and to the doctrine (I Timothy 4:16). The Scriptures are replete with the importance of doctrine. To see how indispensable doctrine is to Christianity, take a Bible concordance and look up the number of times the words "doctrine" and "teaching" are used in the NT. Then you will see the value God places on it. It will astound you.[41]

---

[41] Many translations of the Bible use the word "doctrine," which is from the Latin *doctrina* and means dogmatic teaching. Today, because of the watering down of the evangelical church, the word "doctrine" is considered to be too strong, too offensive. So, a number choose to use the word "teaching," which sounds more pleasant to the unregenerate ear. No matter how you slice it, the Greek word (*didache*) means dogmatic teaching or doctrine.

If there had been no clearly defined membership in the NT churches, those who held false teaching (possibly even cult members) and those with questionable morals could have come among the brethren and created upheaval and division. The weaker and unskilled babes in Christ, in particular, would have been vulnerable to such people as these. Jude warned that corrupt teachers and phony professors had *"crept in,"* seeking to undermine the doctrinal uprightness of the apostolic churches, especially the doctrine of salvation (Jude 3 & 4). If the heretics had been allowed to continue without exposure and discipline, imagine the havoc this would have made of the early churches' testimonies of the Word of God and Christ. Doctrinal integrity is, and must be, maintained in our day through a solid church membership.

Church membership is essential for the church to preserve unity in the body. There can be no true unity of fellowship except they who walk together be in agreement. While you may have unconverted friends in the world, you cannot have genuine fellowship except with those who love, worship, obey, and serve the Lord Jesus Christ. Allowing false teachers, schisms, cults, and people of the world to become part of the church without conversion and membership would only divide and disrupt the unity and fellowship. Preserving the unity of the body is a necessity.

Church membership is essential for the ordering and governing of the congregation. For example, suppose you were in an assembly that decided to follow the scriptural guidelines for officers as found in 1 Timothy 3 and Titus 1. What if an outwardly moral but unbelieving person came into the fellowship and desired to be an officer? Without a scriptural membership in place, this person could not be prevented from becoming an officer and, thus, having oversight in the church's spiritual, business, and monetary affairs. According to the biblical precept and model, in order for one to become an officer in a church, he must be converted (saved), must submit himself to the authority and oversight of the church through membership, and must meet the appropriate qualifications as defined in the Bible. This ensures godly leaders and a well-ordered church.

For the aforementioned reasons, church membership is essential. It is essential for believers' growth and maturity and for the visible assemblies' preservation in their pilgrimages toward God and heaven.

DISCUSSION FOR CHAPTER EIGHT:

1. Explain how the question "Is Church Membership Essential?" can be misleading.

2. What are the two aspects of the Christian life that make church membership essential?

3. Discuss the origin of the word church.

4. How do the twenty-four *"one another"* passages help a church member grow in grace?

5. Why is church membership essential for the local church? (three reasons)

9

WHY SHOULD YOU JOIN A CHURCH?

"I now rejoice in my sufferings for you, and fill up in my flesh what is lacking in the afflictions of Christ, for the sake of His body, which is the church, . . . Him we preach, warning every man and teaching every man in all wisdom, that we may present every man perfect in Christ Jesus."
(Colossians 1:24 & 28)

ACCORDING TO STATISTICIANS, Christianity is reputedly growing in the United States and in many parts of the world. Reports confirming this fact come from different sectors of the globe and, if true, are very encouraging. The Gallup Poll reports that many people in the United States are "born again" or have had some type of "born again" experience. Yet, no matter how much Christianity appears to grow, there is no evidence to suggest a corresponding increase in love for the church, especially in the United States. Individualism is the watchword of the day. People are so wrapped up in their own affairs that the kingdom of God and Christ's churches are neglected. Professing Christians often become so preoccupied with their own problems, trials, difficulties, activities, and recreations that the church is looked upon as being unnecessary, or at least secondary.

As you consider the title of this chapter, I would caution you to recognize that church membership is not for everybody. You may *not* be qualified for membership in one of Jesus Christ's churches! Church membership is only for those who have been truly born again. You must have recognized that you are a helpless sinner before a holy God and have turned from all your known sins and trusted Christ as your Savior and Lord. This is salvation. Unless you have been saved by grace *alone*, through faith *alone*, in the person and work of the Christ Jesus the Lord *alone*, which is also called conversion, you cannot become a member of one of His churches. Conversion to Christ is also described in *Acts 2:47* as the Lord's adding to the church. It was to the visible church in Jerusalem that the Lord *"added"* and verifiable, numerical records were kept (Acts 2:41, 4:4).

If you have been converted and are a true Christian, you are responsible to become a member of a true church of Jesus Christ. You cannot have a consistent walk with God if you are not serious about the church of Jesus Christ. If you are not a member of one of Christ's churches, many parts of the Word of God cannot be applied to your life. This is very serious. The purpose of this chapter is to show you *seven* biblical reasons why you must become a member of a visible church.

WHY SHOULD YOU JOIN A CHURCH?

First, you should join a church because of the relationship between Christ and the church. What is this relationship? You cannot think of Christ without thinking of the church. Christians have an inseparable connection of being *"in Him."* [42]

---

[42] This expression is found over 150 times in the NT and is theologically called "union with Christ."

Individual believers, who form the corporate body of the church, are wonderfully described by the following poem:

> *One in Him before the worlds were framed,*
> *One in Him when He wrote down my name.*
> *One in Christ when He came to earth,*
> *To obey the Law and save from its dearth.*
>
> *One in Him when He died on the Cross,*
> *One when He suffered to redeem my loss;*
> *One in the tomb; one when He arose;*
> *One when He triumphed o'er His foes.*
>
> *One when in Heaven He took His seat,*
> *While seraphs sang all Hell's defeat.*
> *With Him their Head, they stand or fall;*
> *Their Life, their Surety and their All.*[43]

Of all the above-listed connections between Christ and His churches, the most important one is the fact that Christ *loved* the church and gave Himself for it. To love someone involves loving the things he or she loves, and to love Christ involves loving the thing that He loves the most on the earth: the church! To profess love for Christ yet have no love for the church is a great contradiction! Timothy Dwight, a past president of Yale University and grandson of Jonathan Edwards, wrote a hymn about the church to express this point:

> *I love thy kingdom Lord, the house of thine abode,*
> *The church our blest Redeemer saved with His own precious blood.*
>
> *I love thy church O God: her walls before thee stand,*
> *Dear as the apple of thine eye, and graven on thy hand.*

---

[43] Source, author, and date of this poem are unknown.

Jesus Loves the Church and So Should You

For her my tears shall fall, for her my prayers ascend;
To her my cares and toils be giv'n, till toils and cares shall end.

Beyond my highest joy I prize her heavenly ways,
Her sweet communion, solemn vows, her hymns of love and praise.

Do you love the Lord Jesus Christ? Are you a member of a church? If you are not, how can you say you truly love the Savior when you are not a part of that which He loves most on the earth?

Second, you should join a church because of the example of the early Christians. Read carefully *Acts 2:40-47*. This account of the day of Pentecost gives great insight into early Christianity. As Peter finished preaching his memorable sermon, the people were moved in their hearts by the working of God's sovereign Spirit and were converted. Those who received the Word of God and were baptized joined with other believers. This was the normal and natural thing to do. What did this joining involve? It involved continuing under the apostles' preaching and teaching ministry. The new converts did not neglect meeting together for worship and instruction in the Word of God. This joining together also involved fellowship and sharing their lives with other Christians in the church of Jerusalem on a regular basis. It involved a faithful attendance at the ordinance of the Lord's Supper, which is also called the breaking of bread or Communion. Lastly, joining the visible church involved meeting regularly with other church members for corporate prayer. (Again, Acts 2:40-42 gives great insight into the marks of a true church of Jesus Christ.) Have you ever considered what the early Christians did and practiced, and what effects this ought to have on you? Study this passage and consider how you might follow their example.

Third, you should join a church because of apostolic example and practice. Read carefully *Acts 13:1-4 and 14:23, 26-28.* As you progress through the history of the early church as recorded in the book of Acts, you will find the first Christians actively and fervently serving the Lord who had saved them. How were they serving the Lord? In the church! The early believers did not distance themselves from the churches, but became energetically involved in them. As the believers *"ministered unto the Lord"* (in the church), the Holy Spirit did a wonderful thing. He called out from the membership Barnabas and Paul as the first missionaries.

The passage of *Acts 13:1-4* is most instructive with regard to church membership. From the time that Barnabas found Paul and brought him to Antioch to the time the Spirit of God told the church to separate Paul unto a specific work, it was ten years. He had grown in grace and developed in spiritual maturity and giftedness as a member of that visible church until, when it was God's timing, he was sent out to do a greater task. Where was Paul during that ten-year period in Antioch? In a Men's Bible Study? With some Drug Rehabilitation Center? In the local Campus Ministry? (Again, I am opposed to none of these in principle.) No, he was in the church, *"ministering to the Lord."* For ten long years Paul worshipped God, studied, prepared himself, and locally served Christ before being sent out to the regions beyond.

The church at Antioch had publicly recognized officers and leaders (v. 1), which denotes church government. The leadership of the church laid hands on Paul and Barnabas (v. 3), which is ordination. Though Paul was called by the Spirit (v. 2) and sent out by the same (v. 4), it was the church and her leaders that *"sent them away"* (v. 3). These verses show direct

71

church involvement in the formation, recognition, and supervision of missionaries.

The remaining verses of Acts chapters 13 and 14 give a historical description of Paul's first missionary journey. They narrate the activities of Paul and Barnabas as they preached the gospel to those who had never heard it and provided an account of the people who came to Christ and the churches that were planted. It is interesting to note what the apostle and his party did once they had traveled as far as they thought they should. They turned around, retraced their steps, and sought to strengthen the disciples who had settled into the newly-planted churches. As they strengthened the young Christians, the apostles ordained elders (plural) in each local church (singular). This is demonstrated very clearly in Acts 14:23.

When the apostle and his party finished their first missionary tour, where did they go? They returned to Antioch, to the church that had commended them for the work and had sent them—the church where they were members and to which they were accountable. Once the missionaries arrived back home, they gathered the church together to give a report of what God had done through their ministry (Acts 14:26-27). What did Paul do next? The Scripture emphatically states he *"stayed there a long time with the disciples,"* waiting for his next opportunity for official service (Acts14:28). Without a doubt, he immersed himself again into the life of the church until he was sent out once more by the church. When the dispute about circumcision arose, the church in Antioch sent Paul on another assignment to help adjudicate matters at the church in Jerusalem (Acts 15:2-3). This is known as the historic Jerusalem Council. Paul did not go on his own or do his own thing, but was at the bidding and service of his home church.

What does all of this tell us about Paul? He set the NT pattern. His whole Christian life was attached to the church, and his entire ministry as an apostle, in one way or another, was subjugated and absolutely connected to a visible church of which he was a member. Paul and his party were not part of any extraneous groups that circumvented or were not connected with God's *only* heaven-appointed institution. As a Christian, do you desire to be biblical and apostolic? Then you must be formally connected to a visible church, just as the apostles were.

Fourth, you should join a church because it is the *focus* and *context* of the Christian life in the NT epistles. The start of the 21st century exhibits a startling spirit of unbiblical individualism. Again, many professed Christians read their Bibles and think only in terms of themselves as individuals. Yet, the NT's focus is on visible churches comprised of true believers.

Fifth, you should join a church because of the exact and precise NT directive. Read carefully Hebrews 10:23-25. The inspired writer of the book of Hebrews directs and exhorts the Jewish Christians in his day to *"not forsake the assembling of yourselves together, as is the manner of some, but exhorting one another, and so much the more as you see the Day approaching"* (Hebrews 10:25). This type of thinking was not new to these Jewish Christians because the idea was rooted in the Old Testament, especially the book of Psalms. The Old Testament phrases found in the book of Psalms, such as *"house of the LORD," "His temple," "the sanctuary of God," "Your tabernacle," "the courts of the LORD," "the house of God,"* etc., prefigured visible NT churches (Psalms 27:4; 63:2; 73:17; 84:1-4,10; 122:1).

The implications of Hebrews 10:25 are far-reaching. Those who were on the verge of turning away from Christ and going back to Judaism or the world began their departure by staying away from meeting with other believers for worship. The occasional absence increased to frequent absence, finally becoming habitual. Soon these professed Christians stopped attending the meetings for worship altogether. With no godly influence upon them or holy restraint keeping them, those who professed to be saved were soon ensnared by their sins and turned back to false religions and fleshly ways. By turning away from Christ and His people, they were eventually exposed as never having been truly saved when they first professed Christ. They professed Christ, but never possessed Him or His salvation (Hebrews 10:39).

That is why membership in a New Testament church and regular attendance at all of its meetings for worship, prayer, and fellowship are so very important. Once you begin to neglect meeting with the brethren in a biblically ordered church, you will cease to have the godly influence that is needful to help you overcome the world and its temptations. You will not have the brotherly encouragement to continue in the way of Christ. Your soul will become increasingly insensitive to the ways of God, allowing the subtle philosophies of humanistic thinking to dull your mind and pull you farther away from the Word of God. Without God's intervention, this will lead to a departure from the living God and a wrecking of faith. The end result will be no salvation, no eternal life, no heaven, and no God. This does not mean that true believers can lose their salvation, but there will be many at the Last Day who professed faith in Christ, yet were never really saved (Matthew 7:21-23).

"Do not forsake the assembling of yourselves together," says the LORD. How can this precise directive, which is really a *command*, be heeded if you are not a member of a church? It cannot! This

command, along with many others, can have *no* relevance in your life if you are not a member of one of Christ's churches.

Sixth, you should join a church because the Lord Jesus Christ personally and *primarily* interacts with local churches. Read carefully Revelation 2:1 - 3:22. These two chapters deal with the seven churches that were located in Asia Minor, to which the book of Revelation was written. Christ, who is robed in high priestly attire, is set forth in Old Testament imagery as a ministering priest in the temple. Through this Old Testament imagery, the Apostle John presents Christ in the context of worship. He is among (and speaks to) each of these churches, which are represented by lampstands. How does He speak to each of these churches? He speaks to them through the "stars" (i.e., "angels," messengers or pastors of the churches) that are in His right hand (1:20). His control of these church leaders is revealed by the fact that they are represented as being held *in His right hand*, which denotes government and authority. Christ is viewed by the apostle John as standing in the midst of each one of the churches. Though the Savior is with each individual believer, He is especially present with them as they are assembled with, and a part of, a visible church. In His redemptive purposes, Christ interacts *primarily with a church* and not with any other social or religious organization. He is in the midst of each church. How can you know and receive the fullness of the risen, glorified Lord Jesus Christ if you are not a member and part of one of His churches, of which He is in the midst?

Seventh, you should join one of Christ's churches because of the benefits you receive from being a member of it, benefits that you would *not* receive otherwise. God has given these benefits to help you grow as a Christian, to protect and keep you, and to encourage you in every way.

What are some of these benefits? One is pastoral care, which includes spiritual nurturing for your soul and life, by pastors who are called by Jesus Christ to be His undershepherds (1 Thessalonians 5:12; Hebrews 13:7 & 17; 1 Peter 5:2-3). These men of God will help in your trials and difficulties. They will teach and guide you in the Word of God. As they do so, they will be used of God to lead you in Christian maturity and preserve you from falsehood and the Evil One. The church and its God-ordained leaders serve as a bulwark to guard you from apostasy and from going astray. Godly pastors will also assist you in raising your children in the nurture and admonition of the Lord; they will be there as counselors and friends when your children go into hard times and through difficult years.

Another benefit you receive from church membership is the love and service of fellow members. When you join a church, you not only commit yourself to the church, but the church commits itself to you. Brothers and sisters in Christ will lovingly walk side by side with you in all the ups and downs of your Christian life.

The benefits of church membership also include the NT church ordinances. Everyone has heard of baptism and Communion, but few realize that these are for Christians who are members of churches and for them *only*. Baptism is for the new Christian as he enters the Christian life and identifies with the body of Christ. Typically, a new believer becomes a member of a church when he or she is baptized. Communion is for the believer as he continues his walk with Christ as a member of a church (1 Corinthians 11:17-34). Notice in this passage the aspect of *"when you come together as a church"* (v. 18). The benefits of church ordinances will be more fully explained in chapter 11, under THE PUBLIC MEANS OF GRACE.

Yet another benefit of church membership is the provision of an arena in which to exercise spiritual gifts. The local church is the context that grooms us unto holy service for Christ. That is the reason, according to Ephesians 4:7-15 (especially verse 11), that *"pastors and teachers"* were given to the church. These God-called men must meet the qualifications of 1 Timothy 3:1-8 and Titus 1:5-9 and are appointed to equip the body to serve Christ in the church and in the world. A church is a proving ground. Those who are called into gospel service to go outside the church must first prove themselves inside the visible church. They prove that they have the necessary graces and requisite gifts as they busily and sacrificially minister to other church members. Opportunities for greater service do not come to the idle, but to those who faithfully perform their present duties inside this God-ordained arena.

How can these benefits become a part of your Christian walk and spiritual vitality if you are not a member of a true New Testament church? They cannot!

In summary, these *seven* reasons speak clearly as to why you should join a church. Every aspect of the Christian life is vitally attached to a church. Sadly, many professing Christians neglect membership in and assembling with a church of Jesus Christ. When they do so, they founder spiritually and soon make shipwreck of their souls. Trouble and sorrow are their constant companions. Those who bypass the church, or merely interact with it on a casual basis, struggle all their lives. Satan and the affairs of the world constantly buffet them, and they wonder why nothing ever goes right for them. They are like the ember that is removed from the coals of fire. It will glow and give off heat for a very short while, but because of lack of attachment to the fire, it will soon grow cold and die out. You cannot expect to prosper spiritually if you disregard and remain unattached to that which God has ordained. Seek out and become a member of a biblical church of Jesus Christ. You will find blessing and grace as you become obedient to the teaching of God's authoritative and infallible Word.

DISCUSSION FOR CHAPTER NINE:

1. Why do you think that despite the reports of the growth of Christianity, there seems to be no increasing love for the church?

2. Who are the only ones qualified for membership in a visible church?

3. Discuss why you cannot properly think of Christ without thinking of the church.

4. What are the seven reasons you should join a church? Discuss each one.

5. How has this chapter affected your thinking about the church and church membership?

10

WHICH CHURCH SHOULD YOU JOIN?

"And He put all things under His feet,
and gave Him to be head over all things to the church,
which is His body, the fullness of Him who fills all in all."
(Ephesians 1:22-23)

ONCE THE QUESTION of joining a church is settled, the next question is which or what type of church should you join? In looking for a church you should remember the old axiom, "Not everyone who calls himself a Christian is a true Christian." What is true of professed Christians is also true of churches: not every group that calls itself a church is truly a church.

There are certain qualities you should look for in a church. Our purpose is to describe these qualities and thus help you find a true church of Jesus Christ of which you can become a member. The following are qualities you should look for in choosing a church to join:

First, a biblical church is one where the Bible is the only guide for faith and practice. A strong emphasis on preaching and teaching the whole counsel of God demonstrates this. The absence of this emphasis produces an anemic and weak church, one of which you would not want to be a part. The preaching of the Holy Scriptures is the chief means whereby God blesses His people. Titus 1:1-3 says that God has *"manifested His Word through preaching."* Look for and join a church in which the Bible is fully expounded, warmly taught, and practically applied by pastors and elders who are God-called men.

Note also, that many churches today are returning to the historic creeds and confessions of faith of biblical Christianity. They have seen the value of embracing doctrinal standards that confess to the world a summary of the essential beliefs of Holy Scripture. The value of having a confession of faith is fivefold:

1) It is a useful means for the public affirmation and defense of truth;

2) It serves as a public standard of fellowship and discipline;

3) It provides a working manual to teach Christians the cardinal truths of the faith;

4) It serves as a concise standard by which to evaluate ministers of the Word;

5) It contributes to a sense of historical continuity.

The founder of Southwestern Baptist Theological Seminary, B. H. Carroll, has argued the following:

> A church with a little creed is a church with a little life. The more divine doctrines a church can agree on, the greater its power, and the wider its usefulness. The fewer its articles of faith, the fewer its bonds of union and compactness. The modern cry, 'Less creed and more liberty,' is a degeneration from the vertebrate to the jellyfish, and means less unity and less morality, and it means more heresy. Definitive truth does not create heresy—it only exposes and corrects. Shut off the

creed and the Christian world would fill up with heresy unsuspected and uncorrected, but none the less deadly.[44]

Second, you should look for a church where the worship of God is reverent and biblical. There are many churches that seek to entertain people and are more man-centered than God-centered. They feature popular personalities and introduce fashionable elements into worship which the Bible does not allow. You do not go to church primarily to feel better or be entertained, but to worship the true and living God through the Lord Jesus Christ. The basic elements of true worship are reading and exposition of the Scriptures, the Holy Bible; prayer; singing of psalms, hymns, and spiritual songs; giving of tithes and offerings; baptism; and the Lord's Supper. Find a church where these are carried out in holy and joyful reverence to God.

Third, coupled with right worship is the biblical concept of God. The God of the Bible is Spirit, eternal, unchangeable in His being, wisdom, power, holiness, justice, goodness, truth, and love, and is absolutely sovereign and gracious. He must ever be proclaimed and exalted. Any church that is man-centered and holds weak and feeble views of the triune God will not be of much help to you. If there is to be any lasting progress made in the Christian life, a believer must be constantly presented with high and glorious views of God. The belief that God is powerless unless we allow Him to work is an unbiblical and dangerous view of the LORD that produces weak Christians. Remember, the prophet Moses said that God is *"glorious in holiness, fearful in praises, doing wonders"* (Exodus 15:11). A true church is God-centered and always seeking to exalt and please Him.

---

[44] *An Interpretation of the English Bible: Colossians, Ephesians, and Hebrews,* vol. 5, (Grand Rapids: Baker Book House, reprint ed. 1986), p. 140.

You might ask, "How can I comprehend this awe-inspiring God that is revealed in the Bible?" The Apostle Paul says we see *"the knowledge of the glory of God in the face of Jesus Christ"* (2 Corinthians 4:6). That is why a church must be Christ-centered. Therefore, look for a church that has a majestic view of God and is continually lifting up the person and work of the Lord Jesus Christ in all His fullness, offices, and glory.

Fourth, closely aligned with the above is that you should look for a church that is gospel-centered. We are living in unprecedented times that have no parallel in the history of the church. Many mega-churches are known for their monikers of being "seeker-sensitive," "people-driven," or "purpose-driven." If you will notice, there is one thing they have in common: they are man-centered. How foreign is this thinking to that of the first Christian churches and the first Christians. They were gospel-driven, gospel-empowered, and gospel-centered.

What is the gospel? Study very carefully 1 Corinthians 15:1-4 and you will see the clearest definition of the gospel in the entire Word of God. You will quickly observe some things the gospel is not. The gospel is *not* "God loves you and has a wonderful plan for your life"; "the grace of God"; "the power of God"; "the kingdom of God"; "the ABC's" (**A**cknowledge, **B**elieve, **C**onfess); "John 3:16: The Gospel in a Nutshell"; "Jesus is my friend"; or, simply, "good news." Make no mistake, the gospel is good news, but it is more than that: it is the greatest news ever revealed from heaven to mankind.

In studying the previously given passage (vv. 1-3a), you will find certain clauses that qualify the gospel: it is to be preached (v. 1a - proclaimed, heralded); it is to be received (v. 1b); it is that in which believers stand (v. 1c); it is the means *by* which sinners are saved (v. 2a);[45] it is that in which there must be perseverance (v. 2b - "if"); it is something that can be believed in vain (v. 2c - "an empty profession without actually possessing Christ"); and, finally, it is the *only* message which has been divinely revealed (v. 3a). F.W. Grosheide accurately states, "The word 'gospel' is qualified by various clauses, which do not touch upon the content of the gospel, as is done in vs. 3, but which predicate something of the gospel and thus point out its value."[46]

Immediately following these qualifying clauses, Paul gives the content of the gospel (vv. 3b-4). Three branches form the tree of the gospel. *"Christ died for our sins according to the Scriptures"* is the first branch. Observe that Paul does not simply say "Christ died" or "Christ died for you." He emphatically declares that Christ died for *"our sins."* Our sins, which are a transgression of God's holy Law (1 John 3:4; cf. Romans 3:19-20), are what separate humanity from the thrice holy God. Someone had to pay the penalty to remove that great separating barrier. Christ paid that penalty (i.e., wages) of sin in dying for "our sins." The second branch is *"and that He was buried,"* signifying He really died and satisfied God's justice. The burial of Christ, which was in a borrowed tomb, fulfilled the last part of His humiliation.[47] The crowning work of Christ, and the third branch of the gospel tree, is His resurrection from the dead: *"and that He rose again the third day according to the Scriptures."* Paul wonderfully

---

[45] "*By* does not indicate here the ultimate efficient cause, but the means through which something is brought about. [i.e.,] The gospel itself does not save, but God saves by the gospel." F. W. Grosheide, *1 Corinthians*, (Grand Rapids: Wm. B. Eerdmans Publishing Co., 1979), p. 347.

[46] Ibid., 347.

[47] Theologians often speak of Christ's work in two parts — His humiliation and His exaltation. His humiliation was from His birth to His burial. His exaltation began with His resurrection, will culminate at His second (2nd) Coming, and will extend throughout all eternity.

declares that Jesus our Lord *"was delivered up for our offenses, and raised for our justification"* (Romans 4:25). This foundational and indispensable message must be the heart and driving passion of every church true church of Christ.

Fifth, in looking for a church to join, you should seek one where there is love for the brethren (John 13:34-35; 15:9-12; 1 John 4:7 ff.). The Lord Jesus said, *"By this all will know that you are my disciples, if you have love for one another"* (John 13:35). Where people are joined together by love of God's truth there will be love for the brothers and sisters in Christ. Love for the brethren is shown toward each member of the church through actions as well as words. Gossip, backbiting, criticism, and the like, will not be found. Instead, there will be fellowship and an open and shared life with one another. Love for Christ, which stimulates love for those whom Christ loves, will abound.

Sixth, look for a church which has an evident compassion for the unsaved. This will be seen on a local level in works of evangelism and mercy and on a global level in a burden for missions and church planting. The first petition of the Lord's Prayer is for God's name to be hallowed. A church is to strive to make God's saving name and truth known in all the earth so that He, the triune God, may be revered and worshipped by all. Any church that neglects this, especially as it is expressed in the last command of Jesus Christ to go and make disciples of all nations (Matthew 28:18-20; Mark 16:15-16; Luke 24:44-49), is not obedient to God and should not be joined.

Seventh, church discipline is another important criterion in looking for a church to join. Most churches today do not care how their members live and behave, either in public or private, or with one another. Financial and sexual scandals, plus other public transgressions and personal atrocities, abound in many churches; and very little, if anything, is done about them. However, a true church of Jesus Christ will pursue genuine holiness among its members and seek to correct and help those who stray. The church will endeavor to follow the guidelines laid down by the Chief Shepherd, the Lord Jesus Christ, regardless of how unpopular they are to the world and even to other Christians. Join only a church where discipline is practiced in accordance with the following passages: Matthew 18:15-20; 1 Corinthians 5:1-13; 2 Thessalonians 3:6-15; 2 Corinthians 2:5-9. Note carefully, 1 Corinthians 5:1-13 teaches *six* important truths regarding church discipline:

1. Church discipline is not contrary to grace and love. In fact, *not* to implement church discipline may be one of the most unloving things a church can do.

2. The church has a set of rules by which to live (vv. 1-2 & 11).

3. The church is to actually judge its members (vv. 3-5; cf. 1 Timothy 1:20; 2 Timothy 2:16).

4. It is the responsibility of the church to remove the contaminating source of sin (vv. 6-8).

5. Ultimately, when a church exercises its final act of discipline upon its members (excommunication), it withdraws its most precious gift—fellowship (vv. 9-11).

6. Failure of the church to purge the disobedient and unrepentant is flagrant disobedience to God and His holy Word (vv. 12-13).[48]

---

[48] These points are from handwritten notes taken during an expository sermon preached on this passage by the Rev. Jim Elliff of Oklahoma. The sermon was preached in Shreveport, Louisiana; I am not certain of the date or year.

Eighth, look for a church where you will be encouraged and stirred to grow in grace, holiness, love, and Christlikeness. A genuine mutual ministry will involve each member warning the unruly, comforting the fainthearted, upholding the weak ones, and being patient with one another (1 Thessalonians 5:14). This will produce an environment that will strengthen you and cause you to grow as a Christian.

You may not find a church in your neighborhood that possesses all of these qualities. Religious humanism and pragmatism have caused many churches that once stood for truth to abandon biblical principles and guidelines. You may have to travel a distance to find a biblical and suitable congregation of God's people. The travel will be more than worth the trouble as you experience spiritual growth and maturity.

Finally, consider what one writer has said:

> One of the greatest needs of our times is for living, biblical churches. No other institution can adequately replace them. Every Christian ought to give much thought and prayer to this subject, and then order his life in such a way as to further the work of God's true churches. This is not a time for an apathetic, easy-going attitude toward churches. The needs are great. The pressures of ungodliness are heavy. Those who demean God's churches are legion. Let us, then, rise up and go forth with boldness to declare ourselves servants of the God and Father of our Lord Jesus Christ, by following His will in His local church wherever His providence directs us.[49]

There is no such thing as a perfect church; however, to the praise of God, there are good and reforming churches that have

---

[49] Daniel E. Wray, *The Importance Of The Local Church*, (Edinburgh: The Banner of Truth Trust, 1990), p. 15, [note this soon to be re-published by Solid Ground].

rediscovered the previously mentioned truths. When you find a good church, become a member and participate in it whole-heartedly. Support it in every way and labor to make it a useful instrument in the kingdom of God. Pray for its leaders, intermingle with its members, take part in its endeavors, and practice biblical churchmanship to the fullest extent of your God-given ability and ransomed powers.

DISCUSSION FOR CHAPTER TEN:

1. Discuss why it is that not every professed Christian is a true Christian and why every professed church is not a true church.

2. What is the chief means that God uses to bless His people?

3. Talk about the value of having a confession of faith and the five reasons listed.

4. Discuss is the significance of each element of true worship.

5. How do you think modern churches that refuse to exercise church discipline against unrepentant offenders have been hurt in their witness to the world?

6. How do these eight reasons for joining a church fit into your thinking of the Bible?

7. Do you think driving a distance to be a member of a good and biblical church is worth the trouble? Why or why not?

11

WHAT ARE THE "MEANS OF GRACE" IN THE CHURCH?

". . . but grow in the grace and knowledge
of our Lord and Savior Jesus Christ.
To Him be the glory both now and forever. Amen."
(2 Peter 3:18)

THE CHRISTIAN LIFE is a wonderful experience. It begins by a supernatural work of God's unmerited grace in one's heart and life. The Spirit of God applies the work of Christ on the cross to many who are spiritually dead. He regenerates them and brings them to repentance from sin and to faith in the Lord Jesus Christ. This is called salvation. Salvation is a glorious work of God's grace and almighty Spirit.

People often ask what happens after a person is born again and begins the Christian life. Once God saves someone, does He then leave that person to make it into His holy presence in heaven on his own by the works of his flesh? "No!" says Paul the Apostle in Galatians, *"Are you so foolish? Having begun in the Spirit are you now being made perfect by the flesh?"* (Galatians 3:3).

The Christian life begins in grace, by God's sovereign Spirit, and is continued in the same manner. This, however, does not negate activity on the part of the believer. On the contrary, the Word of

God plainly declares that those who are saved are "*. . . created in Christ Jesus unto good works, which God prepared beforehand*" that the Christian "*should walk in them*" (Ephesians 2:10), and they are to work out their salvation in "*fear and trembling*" for God is working in them "*both to will and do of His good pleasure*" (Philippians 2:12-13). (NOTE: The latter verse, which is grossly misused by the cults, does not teach salvation by works. Rather, it is one of the many verses that shows salvation to be totally by grace.) Furthermore, Christians are told to actively "*grow in the grace and knowledge of our Lord and Savior Jesus Christ*" (2 Peter 3:18).

What has the good and gracious God of heaven given to His believing people to help them work out their own salvation, to do the good works which He has ordained, and to grow in grace? God has given specific things to accomplish these desired results. They are what pastors and theologians call the "means of grace."

When the means of grace are active in you, you will see astounding results in your life: spiritual growth, maturity, holiness, joy, and Christlikeness. As these qualities are activated in your life, there will be increased communion and fellowship with God the Father, the Son, and the Holy Spirit. You will be warmed and encouraged in walking with Christ. Spiritual strength and power to overcome temptation, sin, and Satan will be given to you. Help beyond description will be yours in every aspect of the Christian life.

WHAT ARE THE MEANS OF GRACE?

The Oxford American Dictionary defines the word "means" as "that by which a result is brought about." Thus, the means of grace are channels by which God conveys His blessings to people and strengthens them in their Christian life. The Westminster Larger Catechism defines the means of grace as "the outward and ordinary means whereby Christ communicates to His Church the benefits of His mediation [i.e. death]."

To illustrate this, think of a lawn or garden water hose. A hose is not special in itself, but it is the channel through which life-giving and refreshing water flows. So it is with the means of grace. In and of themselves they are not saving or special. However, because Christ ordained and commanded them to be observed, they are special. They are the avenues and channels through which God's life-giving and refreshing blessings flow. Through the means of grace, God imparts strength, peace, comfort, instruction, direction, reproof, rebuke, joy, and many other things that are needful for the Christian life.

While the term "means of grace" is not found in the Bible, it is nevertheless a proper designation of that which is taught in the Bible. There are two types of means of grace: private and public.

WHAT ARE THE PRIVATE MEANS OF GRACE?

*THE **FIRST** PRIVATE MEANS of grace is reading the Word of God.* God has given a book in which He speaks to us. God no longer speaks in an audible voice, as in times past, but speaks through His Son (Hebrews 1:1-4); and His Son, Christ Jesus, speaks to us in the Holy Scriptures, the Bible. It is in the sacred pages of His Word that He speaks with a voice that can wake the dead and give life.

The Holy Bible was written by holy men of God as they were inspired (1 Timothy 3:16) and carried along by the Holy Spirit (2 Peter 1:21). It is a perfect treasure of heavenly instruction and knowledge. God is its author, salvation its end, and truth without any mixture of error its content. The Bible principally teaches what people are to believe about God and what duty God requires of them. It reveals the principles by which God will judge humanity; and it is the supreme standard by which all human creeds, conduct, and opinions should be tested. Hear what J.C. Ryle says:

> Make it a part of every day's business to read and meditate on some portion of God's Word. Yesterday's bread will not feed the laborer today, and today's bread will not feed the laborer tomorrow. Gather your manna fresh every morning. Choose your own seasons and hours. Do not scramble over and hurry your reading. Give your Bible the best, and not the worst, of your time. *Read all of the Bible and read it in an orderly way.* I fear there are many parts of the Word which some people never read at all. To this habit may be traced that lack of broad, well-proportioned views of truth, which is so common in this day. I believe it is by far the best plan to begin in the Old and New Testaments at the same time, - to read each straight through to the end and then begin again. *Read the Bible in a spirit of obedience and self-application.* Sit down to the study of it with a daily determination that you will live by its rules, rest on its statements, and act on its commands. That Bible is read best which is practiced most.[50]

This is the means whereby God speaks to His people. As we read the Bible, God speaks to us, blesses us, and strengthens us with all that we need for our daily walk.

*The **second** private means of grace is prayer.* What is prayer? Prayer is one way in which the Christian cultivates a living relationship

---

[50] *Practical Religion*, (Cambridge, England: James Clarke & Co. Ltd., 1977), pp. 95-96.

with the living God. Prayer in personal and daily devotions is indispensable. It involves talking to and communing with God. In this communion we offer up our heartfelt desires. It is one way we as believers converse "face to face" with God. The Old Testament gives numerous examples: Genesis 18:23 ff.; Exodus 5:22, 6:1,10,12,28-30; Deuteronomy 3:23-26; Psalm 27:8. The New Testament summarizes the same in Acts 13:1-2.

Asking God for the good things He has promised is a vital part of prayer (Matthew 7:7,11; Luke 11:5-13; Colossians 1:9-12; James 1:5,6). According to Philippians 4:6-7, prayer is a key to a Christian's experiencing God's peace. It is also the means by which the believer surrenders his or her will to God. (See the Lord Jesus' example in Matthew 26:39, 42, 44.)

There are several elements of prayer. Prayer may include one or more of the following: adoration and praise, thanksgiving, confession of sin, supplication, intercession, and consecration of self to God.

According to Ephesians 6:18 and Jude 20, prayer is to be in the Spirit. The Holy Spirit is the one who helps Christians pray. He attests to the spirits of believers that they are the children of God and causes them to cry out "Abba, Father" (Romans 8:15; Galatians 4:6). He prompts Christians to pray by bringing to mind the words and promises of the Lord Jesus Christ (John 14:26). He also burdens hearts for others (Romans 10:1, cf. 9:1-2). Therefore, when you do not feel like praying, ask God the Holy Spirit to help you pray.

Christ has given His people a pattern to help them pray. It is often called The Lord's Prayer and is found in *Matthew 6:9-13* and *Luke 11:1-4*. This pattern of prayer was not given to be recited as a ritual in private or in public worship. Reciting this prayer does not discharge your obligation to pray. Instead, Christ gave it to teach believers how to pray properly. There are six petitions in the prayer. The first three deal with God's priorities and the last three address our needs. In this pattern, Christ is teaching that before we should pray for our needs, we must *first* pray for God's priorities.

*The **last** private means of grace is meditation.* After the Christian has come into the presence of God by reading the Scriptures and praying, he nurtures what he has received by meditating. Thomas Watson, one of the Puritans, has said that, "Meditation is like the watering of the seed, it makes the fruits of grace to flourish." What digestion is to the body, meditation is to our soul. C.H. Spurgeon gave good instruction when he said the following:

> Our bodies are not supported by merely taking food into the mouth, but the process which really supplies the muscle, and the nerve, and the sinew, and the bone, is the process of digestion. It is by digestion that the outward food becomes assimilated with the inner life. And so it is with our souls; they are not nourished merely by what we hear going hither and thither, and listening awhile to this and then to that, and then to the other. Hearing, reading, marking, and learning, all require inwardly digesting; *and the inward digesting of the truth lies in the meditating upon it.*[51]

The attitude of the psalmist David was, *"I will **meditate** on Your precepts, and contemplate Your ways. I will delight myself in Your statutes; I will not forget Your Word"* (Psalm 119:15-16). He knew the value

---

[51] Copied from a brochure printed by Christian Discount Book Company, a business now defunct.: nd.

of meditation as a private means of grace some 1,000 years before Christ was born.

WHAT ARE THE PUBLIC MEANS OF GRACE?

*ASSEMBLING TOGETHER FOR WORSHIP is the **first** public means of grace.* God never intended the true believer to live the Christian life alone. After Christ's ascension, the apostles went everywhere starting churches and ordaining elders in each (as studied earlier). They did this so the young Christians could be strengthened, encouraged, guided, instructed, and, above all, so that they could worship God together. God, not man, ordained that by publicly assembling for worship every Lord's Day, each believer would receive divine help and blessing for the days ahead. Together the people of God would not only receive God's benediction, but they would mutually fortify one another. Christians are commanded not to forsake the assembling of themselves together in public worship (Hebrews 10:25).

Historically, Christian churches have always worshipped on Sunday. It was on Sunday, the first day of the week, that the Lord Jesus rose from the dead and secured the fall of Satan's empire. Christ met with His apostles on two successive Sundays after His resurrection. Fifty days later, at Pentecost, again on the first day of the week, the Holy Spirit came as a mighty rushing wind, filling and empowering the church. Since then, Christians have met on Sunday—the first, best, and brightest of days—to worship the first, best, and brightest of beings, the LORD God of hosts and His Son Jesus Christ (Acts 20:7; 1 Corinthians 16:2).[52]

---

[52] The early Church, the Protestant Reformers, and the early Baptists consider Sunday to be the Christian Sabbath, as opposed to Saturday, the Jewish Sabbath. See *LBC*, 22:1-8.

The elements of public worship are public reading of Scripture combined with the proclamation of the Word; singing of psalms, hymns, and spiritual songs; giving of tithes and offerings; and prayer. In the reading and exposition of the Scripture, God speaks to us; in the singing, giving, and praying, we speak to God. While each of these elements of worship is important, the preaching of the Word of God is the most important. Our forefathers realized this when they wrote the following:

> The Spirit of God makes the reading, *but especially the preaching of the Word of God*, an effectual means of convincing and converting sinners, *and of building them up in holiness and comfort* through faith unto salvation (*The Baptist Catechism*, Q. 93).

*The ordinances of the gospel, a part of corporate worship, are the **second** public means of grace.* An ordinance is a custom and practice ordained by the Lord Jesus Christ while on the earth to be practiced by His churches until He comes again. In the true churches of Jesus Christ there are only two ordinances: baptism and the Lord's Supper.

Baptism is the first ordinance *instituted* by the Lord Jesus Christ while on the earth. He commanded it to be performed by His apostles and churches until the end of the world (see Matthew 28:18-20). A professed believer who has neglected this, Christ's first command, has no right to call himself a Christian. Baptism is to be performed by total immersion in water, in the name of the Father, and of the Son, and of the Holy Spirit.

Baptism is reserved only for believers. It is not for unbelieving infants. There is not one instance of infant baptism seen in the NT, and no commandment for such is ever found. It has

always been for those who repent and believe and are thus converted and saved (see Acts 2:41, 18:8). This ordinance was designed to be a picture of regeneration and a testimony to the world that we are followers of Christ. It also serves to strengthen our resolve to follow Him. It is taking the name of Christ as our own.

The Lord's Supper, or Communion, is the second ordinance *instituted* by the Lord Jesus while on the earth. It is a divinely appointed means of strengthening the faith of believers. The Lord's Supper is not a sacrifice offered to God, but only a commemoration of that one-time offering up of the Lord Jesus Christ Himself, on the cross, for sins. As often as the Lord's Supper is observed, it is to be *"in remembrance of Him"* (1 Corinthians 11:24-26). The observance of this ordinance should **never** be missed unless one is providentially hindered!

The elements of the Lord's Supper—bread and wine—are symbols. Each element represents a specific aspect of Christ's atonement. The bread symbolizes the bruised and crushed body of the Savior, broken for our sin. The wine symbolizes the blood of Christ, shed for the cleansing of our sin. There is nothing magical about the bread and wine. They do *not* change and become the literal, physical body and blood of Christ, but remain what they are.[53]

A careful study of the Scriptures reveals the requirements for partaking of the Lord's Supper. The person *must* be one who is a true convert to Christ, baptized, seeking to walk in a way

---

[53] This is contrary to the Roman Catholic doctrine of *transubstantiation*, which teaches that the bread and the wine of the mass actually change into the substance of Christ's literal, physical body and blood.

pleasing to God, and a member of one of Christ's visible churches. Remember, this ordinance was not given to individual Christians, but to churches and their members.

*Fellowship with brothers and sisters in Christ is the **third** public means of grace.* God's people come from all types of background. Yet, one thing unites them all: they are in Christ! Christ loved them with an everlasting love and drew them with lovingkindness. All barriers fall before the electing, redeeming, saving love of Christ (Ephesians 2:14-16).

Fellowship means "share together" or "shared life," especially as it relates to other Christians. When Christ saved you He did not intend you to live in isolation. You were meant to be a part of one of Christ's churches and to enjoy fellowship with other believers (see Acts 2:41-42). One of the most blessed things you realized after your conversion is the bond you have with true Christians.

Fellowship is not Christians' socializing about sports, hobbies, weather, jobs, or politics, although there is no harm in talking about these matters. Instead, it is the shared heart and life with one another in the things of the Lord Jesus and His Word. The uniqueness of Christian fellowship lies in being able to talk about and share together the joys, happiness, victories, problems, trials, sorrows, temptations, and blessings of our walk with God. Proverbs 27:17 says, *"As iron sharpens iron, so a man sharpens the countenance of his friend."* Fellowship with Christians in a local church is iron sharpening iron. Fellowship with brothers and sisters in Christ is a means of grace to keep us spiritually sharp and healthy.

*Corporate prayer (Acts 2:42) is the **fourth** public means of grace.* The early churches not only continued in the apostles' doctrine, the Lord's Supper, and in fellowship, but they were faithful in *prayer* (i.e., praying together as a group). Church gatherings for prayer was one way of bearing one another's burdens and fulfilling the law of Christ (Galatians 6:2). In the book of Acts are examples of the early Christians praying together. On the day of Pentecost, what were the believers doing? Praying! (1:12-14, cf. 2:1). Through the means of corporate prayer, the church saw the Lord God deliver them from the hand of their enemies (4:23-33). Peter was set free from prison because the church prayed together (12:5). The history of the New Testament churches is a picture of the blessing and necessity of prayer meetings.

All that is true of private prayer is true of public prayer, with the exception that public prayer is of the corporate body. If God is with His people and blesses them individually with His presence, how much more is this true when the church comes together for worship and prayer? If He hears and answers the prayers of one, how much more will He hear and answer the prayers of many? One of the Puritans, David Clarkson, has said, "The presence of God, which, enjoyed in private, is but a stream; but in public becomes a river, a river that makes glad the city of God."

A gracious, wise, and loving Father in heaven has given these means to His children for their good (see Deuteronomy 10:13). He has not given them to put you in bondage to man-made rules, but to bless, strengthen, and encourage you. The private means of grace are given for your daily Christian life in a work-a-day world. The public means of grace are given for your benefit within a local church of Jesus Christ. Put each of them into practice right now and watch your Christian life develop, grow, and blossom. Pursuing these God-ordained means will glorify God, increase Christ's kingdom, and bring you godliness, peace, and joy.

DISCUSSION FOR CHAPTER ELEVEN:

1. What is salvation, as described in the first paragraph of this chapter?

2. Discuss the astounding results of the means of grace in the life of a Christian.

3. Give the definition of the word "means" found in the Oxford American dictionary.

4. Why is the order of the private means of grace given as they are?

5. What are the public means of grace and how important are they to the believer?

6. What would you say to someone who has left off or is neglecting the private or public means of grace?

7. How does a Christian active in the means of grace differ from one who is not?

12

WHAT ARE THE PRIVILEGES AND BLESSINGS
OF CHURCH MEMBERSHIP?

*"For God is not the author of confusion but of peace,
as in all the churches of the saints."*
(1 Corinthians 14:33)

SOMEONE HAS SAID, *"Church membership is a privilege to which the world is not invited."* How true this is! Only legitimate disciples are invited to partake in this holy privilege, and they should take every opportunity to avail themselves of the advantages that are theirs as members of a New Testament church.

The *first* of the privileges and advantages of church membership is pastoral oversight and care (1 Thessalonians 5:12; Hebrews 13:7, 17; 1 Peter 5:2-3). As sheep need a shepherd, so the people of God need Christ's undershepherds. God, in His infinite wisdom, ordained it to be this way. What a great privilege it is to have those who are called of God to watch over your souls, care for, steer, guide, and direct you. The most important aspect of pastoral care is the feeding of the flock by means of the nourishing Word of God. In the old days, pastors and elders visited the homes of believers to discern their overall spiritual condition, to aid them in establishing family devotions or worship, and to counsel them in any problems they faced. This was done on a regular basis. There was no haughty or lording spirit in these men; instead, following the apostolic example, they possessed a humble desire to be a helper of the Christian's joy (2 Corinthians 1:24).

Today there is such a spirit of lawlessness that, many times, believers become indignant at even the thought of regular pastoral visitation in the home. People want to be left alone and pastoral care becomes a bother. The church and her pastors are wanted only when there is trouble, illness, death, or marriage. When believers reject the injunctions of Scripture concerning pastoral care, they do great harm to their souls.

The *second* privilege is closely akin to the first: the instruction and watchcare of the children of the church. While there are many hirelings who preach to bring glory to themselves and who care more for filthy lucre than they do for the souls of others, I am glad that Christ has His undershepherds that care for the children as well. Parents find it a joy to have pastors instruct and reinforce what is taught at home. Nothing can replace pastors and elders who have a yearning desire to see children brought to a saving knowledge of Christ.

The *third* privilege of membership is the love and service received from fellow church members. Someone has said, "When a believer is received into church membership, not only does he pledge himself to the church, but the church pledges itself to him." When we see that we have many brothers and sisters in Christ who will love and care for us and be servants to us, it should cause us to be humble and thank God for this privilege of church membership.

New Testament church ordinances, especially the Lord's Supper, are the *fourth* privilege of membership. No one who refuses to affiliate with a local body of Jesus Christ has the right to partake of the ordinances of baptism and communion. The Lord's Supper, as expounded in 1 Corinthians 11:17-34, is given to the visible church and to it *only!*

Numerous radio and television evangelists, in order to solicit funds, play upon the emotions of disobedient and uncommitted "Christians" by celebrating communion via prerecorded programs. They record the programs in such places as Israel and mail out the cups and bread for home participants. By doing this, they are desecrating this holy ordinance and Christ's body in particular. The visible churches *alone* have been given the stewardship of these ordinances, which God has ordained to strengthen believers.

The *last* privilege and advantage of membership is the provision of an arena in which to exercise spiritual gifts. Upon conversion, each Christian is endowed with certain spiritual gifts (Romans 12:3ff.; Ephesians 4:7ff.; 1 Peter 4:10,11). These gifts, conferred by Christ, the Head of the church, are not for personal edification or boasting, but for serving one another in the body of Christ. ". . .[E]very believer," says Professor Donald Macleod, "has *charismata* with which he is expected to serve the body of Christ." He continues with the following:

> All do not have the same gifts, either as to number or as to eminence. God distributes to each according to His sovereign will. But none can regard himself as useless or redundant. Each member has a meaningful role within the body of Christ. Without his contribution, the body is impoverished—[54]

---

[54] *The Promise of the Spirit* (Rosshire, Scotland: Christian Focus Publications, 1986), p. 46.

God has ordained that spiritual gifts be exercised within the arena of the visible church. There is much service to be done using the gifts of Christ, both in an informal and formal church setting. Informally, there are many brethren who need help in a multitude of ways. Formally, there is a great need for godly pastors, elders, deacons, and missionaries.

Many are laboring in Christian service without being sent. In numerous instances, men and women mistake a fanciful whim or a sudden emotional feeling for a call of God. They go into the pastoral ministry or onto the mission field possessing a zeal without knowledge; rather than bringing honor and glory to Christ, they quickly and unknowingly become instruments of the devil to dishonor the Lord. Those who have submitted themselves to a church will have many opportunities to exercise their gifts under the spiritual and wise counsel of men of God. When they have proven themselves within the domain of the church, they will be given greater avenues of service outside the confines of their own congregation.

NOTE: C.H. Spurgeon, in his book, *Lectures To My Students*, gives four ways one can know if he has been called into the ministry. One of the four is if the individual edifies the people of God. There are many who are knowledgeable and have correct theology, yet when they seek to teach the people of God, they are not a blessing. Rather than submitting themselves to the judgment of the saints and the elders, many often go out on their own to "serve the Lord." If someone has the call of God upon them, it will soon become evident to God's people. Then, when recognized and called to a place of ministry (whether in an established work or a mission field setting) they will have the authority of Christ and the church to stand behind them.[55]

God the Lord has bestowed these great privileges and advantages upon His churches to enrich Christ's people. The world knows nothing of these mercies. Do not be like world and remain outside of a visible church of Jesus Christ.

DISCUSSION FOR CHAPTER TWELVE:

1. Why is the world not invited to partake of the privilege of church membership?

2. What connection does Hebrews 13:17 have with pastoral watchcare?

3. How is the second privilege closely akin to the first?

4. Should someone be allowed to partake in communion when he or she has not obeyed Christ's command to be baptized?

5. Is the ordinance of the Lord's Supper given to local churches or individual believers?

6. Why is it important for the Christian to exercise his or her spiritual gifts within the arena of the local church?

---

[55] Lecture II. The Call to the Ministry, (Pasadena, TX: Pilgrim Publications, 1990).

13

WHAT ARE THE RESPONSIBILITIES
OF CHURCH MEMBERSHIP?

"For the time has come for judgment to begin at the house of God;
and if it begins with us first,
what will be the end of those who do not obey the gospel?"
(1 Peter 4:17)

PRIVILEGES AND ADVANTAGES go hand in hand with responsibilities. The LORD has given many gracious privileges and advantages that, if we partake of them, make us accountable and responsible to Him and each other. The following responsibilities are *not* listed in order of importance.

The **first** responsibility of church membership is loyalty to the church. By loyalty to the church, I mean fidelity to the teachings of the church as far as they are loyal to the Word of God. Many churches have drawn up articles of faith, and, as stated earlier, some have returned to the historical church confessions of faith. (A good number of Baptists have returned to and embraced the historical *London Baptist Confession of Faith of 1689*.) Local churches believe these articles or confessions of faith to be no more than accurate *expressions* of the system of doctrine taught in the Bible. They do not believe them to be inspired. The value of a confession of faith is that it can be used as ". . .

an assistance to you in controversy, a confirmation in faith, and a means of edification in righteousness." These words are just as valuable today as when C.H. Spurgeon wrote them in 1855, when he republished the "*1689*" for his congregation. It is only right, then, for a church to ask someone who desires to be a member to be loyal to its doctrinal position as defined in its statement or confession of faith.

Attendance at all church meetings is *another* responsibility of church membership (This will be studied further in the next chapter.) The very first church is described with the words *"continued steadfastly"* (Acts 2:42), denoting a consistent, regular attendance to the apostles' doctrine, fellowship, the breaking of bread, and prayers. These all occurred in the context of public assembling and worship. As the first Christians and members of the first church faithfully attended *all* church meetings, so should the members of all of Christ's churches 2,000 years later.

Some members absent themselves from meeting with God's people because there is a speaker who is not particularly enjoyed, because an unpalatable subject is being taught, or because a business meeting is deemed unimportant, etc. Add to these a host of other reasons such as work, family, recreation, and the like. None of these excuses are acceptable in the sight of God, the Judge of all. Regardless of the situation, unless providentially hindered, a church member is responsible to attend all stated meetings. Saving Christianity cannot be separated from public worship with Christ's people on the Lord's Day and assembling together with them at additional times!

A *third* responsibility lies in the matter of financial giving (1 Corinthians 16:2; 2 Corinthians 8:9). Giving is requisite so the congregation can support its officers, take care of necessary expenses, sustain benevolence and works of charity, and carry on the work of missions and the cause of Christ around the world. Some resent the idea of giving money, but the Scriptures teach that believers should give at least ten percent of their total income (Malachi 3:8-10, cf. 1 Corinthians 16:1-2; Matthew 23:23). How little Christians give to the LORD'S church and work in proportion to that which Christ has given them!

People err when they look upon giving as a burden, rather than an act of worship. In 2 Corinthians 8, the incentive Paul used to motivate believers to give was spiritual. He did not resort to carnal or fleshly motives. Often one hears, "If you will give, you will be rich and prosperous," or "If you give, the LORD will return to you fourfold." Many play upon the lusts and emotions of others, but not so with the inspired apostle. In verse 9 we find, *"For you know the grace of our Lord Jesus Christ, that though He was rich, yet for your sakes He became poor, that you through His poverty might become rich."* Paul simply reminded the church members at Corinth of the sacrificial and propitiatory gift of Christ on the cross for sinners. This will always stir the redeemed of the LORD to give.

If Christian giving is looked upon as a matter of worship, instead of a drudgery, it will turn into a delightful joy. You should say in your heart each time you give, "O Father, I thank You for being gracious to me. Accept this gift, small and insignificant as it is. Receive it as a token of my worship and praise for the great sacrifice that You made for me in sending the Lord Jesus Christ to become poor and die in my stead on the cross." This is the correct and proper attitude in giving.

Mutual ministry is *another* responsibility of church membership. Many people think the pastors and elders are the only ones who are to labor and serve Christ in the church. This is unbiblical thinking. God speaks otherwise in 1 Thessalonians 5:11-14. In verses 11-13, Paul admonishes the brethren in the church to comfort themselves together and edify one another. He continues in verse 14 by urging them, ". . . *warn those who are unruly, comfort the fainthearted, uphold the weak, be patient with all.*" No one lives unto himself and no one dies unto himself! Brethren must be built up and comforted. The unruly and straying ones must be warned. The feebleminded among you must not be despised, but consoled. The weak must be supported. This is not the responsibility of the pastors, only, but of each church member. Those who are redeemed are their brother's keeper!

A **fifth** responsibility of church membership is to minister to the ones primarily responsible for ministering to the body: the pastors and elders. As an individual member, you are to pray for those who have pastoral oversight over you. They are not "super men," but servants of God who wrestle with weaknesses, temptations, and sins, just as you do. You must encourage and honor these men of God because of their office and call. Along with this, you must provide financially for them. This is seen in 1 Timothy 5:17-18: *"Let the elders who rule well be counted worthy of double honor, especially those who labor in the word and doctrine. For the Scripture says, `You shall not muzzle an ox while it treads out the grain,'* and, *'the laborer is worthy of his wages'."* (cf. 1 Corinthians 9:13-14). For the church member not to pray for, encourage, honor, and provide for those who give themselves *"continually to prayer and the ministry of the Word"* is a sin against Christ, who placed these gifted men in His church.

The **last** responsibility of church membership is evangelism and witnessing. Someone has said the following:

Every believer is to be a witness for Christ. He is to tell others of the work of Christ and also to give his own personal testimony about what Christ has done for him. We should witness in the shop, in the office, on the street, at school, in our homes, and wherever God may place us. Evangelism is not the exclusive occupation of a few, but the blessed privilege of every believer.[56]

This is not only to glorify God and save souls, but to enlarge the church as well. If church members do not evangelize, the church will soon grow introverted, wither, and die. These responsibilities are not unreasonable, but scriptural; since they are such, each Christian must of necessity obey all of them!

DISCUSSION FOR CHAPTER THIRTEEN:

1. Describe loyalty to the church and its extent.

2. What part does Hebrews 10:25 play in the active participation of church membership?

3. Discuss the proper attitude a believer should have in financial giving. Also, why is it necessary to give?

4. Review 1 Thessalonians 5:14 and discuss what part you can have in mutual ministry.

5. What are the ways you can minister to those pastors and elders who continually minister to you?

6. What will happen to a church if its members do not evangelize?

---

[56] Ernest Pickering, *The Theology of Evangelism* (Clarks Summit: Bible Baptist College Press, 1974), p. 46.

14

IS CHURCH ATTENDANCE REALLY IMPORTANT?

"For a day in Your courts is better than a thousand.
I would rather be a doorkeeper
in the house of my God than to dwell in the tents of wickedness."
(Psalm 84:10)

WHAT DO YOU DO, as a Christian, when terrible things come upon you? When tragedies, calamities, sorrows, and heartaches visit your home? When you feel tempted to go back to the pleasures of the world? When you become depressed and do not even want to see or talk with anyone? When you become so discouraged that you would just like to "give up"? When financial setbacks hit you? When your heart is filled with envy at the successes of others? When you think that nobody understands, likes, or even cares about you? When you feel inferior and imagine that you are the worst person on the earth? When you are filled with fear over what others think about you? When you are angry at a brother or sister in Christ whom you believe has wronged you? When on a Saturday night you are tired and exhausted from the pressures of a week of work or school? When on a Sunday afternoon the demands of work or school cry out for immediate attention? When it seems that God has utterly abandoned you and you do not sense or "feel" His presence? When it feels like your whole world is going to cave in? What do you do during these times and hundreds of other situations like them? What do you do?

Trying times, like the above, are not unique to us who live at the opening of the 21st century. God's people throughout all the ages have experienced trials equal to those you face. While the centuries and cultural surroundings are different, the reality and intensity of the situations are the same. Their minds and hearts have thought and felt exactly what yours have.

There are many *natural* responses when difficulties arise. However, there are two responses that are the most common. The first is to become dismayed. The basic Hebrew meaning of the word *"dismayed"* is to "lie down." Thus, the temptation during trying times is to lie down, either physically or mentally or spiritually. The LORD God commands us not to lie down (Joshua 1:9). The second *natural* response is to *"forsake the assembling of ourselves"* with other believers in the worship of God at the house of God. Many weary professed Christians simply do not go to church. Because they do not "feel like it," they just do not go.

What should you do? The answer is found in the Psalms in the response of a believer named Asaph. When he faced many of the exact situations you face, he did not simply lie down and fail to go to the house of God (i.e., church). Instead, he declares from a resolute mind and heart:

> *"Your way, O God, is in the **sanctuary**."* (Psalm 77:10a)

> and

> *"When I thought how to understand this, it was too painful for me—until I went into the **sanctuary of God**; then I understood their end."*
> (Psalm 73:15-16)

By *"sanctuary"* and *"sanctuary of God,"* Asaph meant the house of God, the gathering of believers on the Sabbath to worship the triune God—Father, Son, and Holy Spirit. The Psalmist knew the best thing for him was *not* to stay home *or* go for a drive *or* work *or* study *or* do something else that would cause him to absent himself from worshipping the LORD and meeting with the people of God. He knew, despite the way he felt or the pressures on him, that God's *"way"* of blessing was in His house with His people on His Day. It was in the sanctuary of God that Asaph's understanding and thinking were corrected and his emotions and feelings untwisted.

All of us face tempting and trying situations that often distort our thinking and fog our emotions. Trials can cause us to think wrongly and not see things clearly. Our view of life and reality, God's world, and things to come can easily become clouded. Then, like a tangled shoelace, we need to have our thinking unknotted and straightened out.

When hard and trying times, discouragement, and tempting situations come upon you, what do you do? The next time you face them, what will you do? Do not respond naturally. May you, even though you do not feel like going to church and are not thinking rightly, determine to go to the house of God and say, **"*Your way, O God, is in the sanctuary.*"** Then and there you will find blessing.

Not only will you be blessed, but you need to realize that being faithful and consistent in attending a true church of Jesus Christ and in worshipping God is extremely important, more important than you may comprehend. Irregularity and unfaithfulness in attending church conveys a certain message and produces definite short-term and far-reaching effects.

Habitual failure to assemble yourself with Christ's people at all stated meetings for worship, unless you are sick or legitimately hindered, says several things about you:

1. It reveals a cold heart and a lack of fervent love to Christ, who instituted visible churches (Revelation 2:4, 3:20).

2. It shows disregard for the apostolic example and command of God's holy Word (Acts 2:41 ff.; Hebrew 10:25).

3. It robs you of blessing and help for the days ahead.

4. It cheats your fellow Christians of blessings and help they would receive from your ministry to them (1 Thessalonians 5:14; Hebrews 10:24, *"And let us consider how we may spur one another on toward love and good works."* [NIV]).

5. It grieves the Holy Spirit who dwells in each believer individually and in the church as a whole.

6. It steals the joy of pastors who oversee you and minister the Word of God to you (Hebrews 13:7, 17; cf. 1 Thessalonians 5:12-13).

7. It can influence others to become unfaithful, lazy, indifferent, and selfish. Many young Christians have said, "Brother or Sister So-and-So does not come regularly; why should I?" God tells us in His Word that you are a letter known and read by all men (2 Corinthians 3:2-3a).

8. It discourages brethren in the body with whom you are joined because you are not with them. They miss your person and presence.

9. It is a poor testimony to the world of unbelievers (1 John 13:35; cf. 1 John 3:13-14).

10. It demonstrates your lack of vision for the future of the particular church of which you are a member (Jeremiah 29:10-11).

11. It makes you a covenant-breaker in your commitment to God and to the church of which you are a member.

12. It is a dreadful step toward backsliding and apostasy (study Hebrews 10:25 in its context of verses 19-39).

13. It shows disrespect for the best and brightest day of the week—the Lord's Day, the day in which the Lord Jesus rose from the dead (1 Corinthians 16:1-2).

A Christian is saved by grace alone, through faith alone, in Christ alone, and God's saving grace causes one to love Christ and His churches (Psalms 27:4; 84:1-2 & 10; 87:1-3). If there is no love for Christ's churches or no concern to be identified with a visible church, it may be you do not love Christ. Your faith is suspect. True and saving faith creates a love for Christ and the things He loves; He *"loved the church and gave Himself for it"* (Ephesians 5:25). The puritan, John Owen, put it well with the following:

> It is the duty of everyone who professes faith in Jesus Christ, and takes due care of his own eternal salvation, voluntarily and by his own choice to join himself to some particular congregation of Christ's institution. . .no particular person is to be esteemed a legal, true subject that does not appear in these His courts with a solemn homage to Him.[57]

---

[57] *Works*, vol. 15, "Duty of Believers to Join Themselves in Church Order" (Edinburgh: The Banner of Truth Trust, 1979), pp. 319-327.

May each of you say from your heart, as David said of old, *"I was glad when they said to me, Let us go into the house of the LORD"* (Psalm 122:1).

DISCUSSION FOR CHAPTER FOURTEEN:

1. Discuss some of the trying and difficult times people often face.

2. What are two (most common) *natural* responses people often have during trying and difficult times?

3. How did the psalmist Asaph respond?

4. What is meant by the phrase *"sanctuary of God"*?

5. What messages do irregularity and unfaithfulness in church attendance convey about a believer? (13 things)

6. What brought gladness to the heart of the psalmist David?

15

WHAT IS REQUIRED TO BE A CHURCH MEMBER?

"Then those who gladly received his word were baptized;
and that day about three thousand souls were added to them.
And they continued steadfastly in the apostles' doctrine and fellowship,
in the breaking of bread, and in prayers."
(Acts 2:40-41)

AMONG CHURCHES TODAY, even those that have a formal church membership, oftentimes the standards for membership are quite low. Rather than striving for a pure body, churches race to see which can become the biggest and fastest growing. To accommodate this mentality, men devise quick and easy requirements for membership. Biblical requirements are distinctly different from man-made ones.[58] John Owen contrasted the apostolic pattern with modern practice:

> And herein we are remote from exceeding the example and care of the primitive churches; yea, there are but few, if any, that arrive unto it. Their endeavor was to preach unto all they

---

[58] Usually this is done through the "invitation system" or "altar call." This practice has no footsteps or example in the New Testament and is credited to the semi-pelegian evangelist, Charles G. Finney, in the 1820s. My predecessor at the church where I now pastor noted that in Shreveport, Louisiana, on any given Sunday, a serial killer or a pedophile, with an easy profession of faith in Christ and baptism, could join five different churches on the same Sunday and no one would be the wiser.

could, and they rejoiced in the multitudes that came to hear the word; but if any did essay to join themselves unto the church, their diligence in their examination and instruction, their severe inquiries into their conversation, their disposing of them for a long time into a state of expectation for their trial, before their admittance, were remarkable. And some of the ancients complained that the promiscuous admittance of all sorts of persons that would profess the Christian religion into church membership, which took place afterward, ruined all the beauty, order, and discipline of the church.[59]

What then are the true requirements for church membership? **First** and foremost is regeneration (conversion). Regeneration, or the new birth, is evidenced by repentance and faith in Christ. The Savior said in Mark 1:15b, "*. . . repent and believe the gospel.*" The point is well made by Vernon Lyons:

> . . . the basis of Scripture has always held to a regenerate membership, that is a membership that is made up only of people who give a credible profession of faith in Christ. In the apostolic church only those who became believers, those who received the Word of God and who had repented of their sins, and were baptized were received as church members.[60]

Second, a personal confession of faith is required. Before the congregation can welcome individuals into its fellowship, there must be an *observable* testimony of having like precious faith and a *verifiable* declaration that they, also, have passed from death to life. The bond of fellowship within the assembly is greatly

59 *Works*, vol. 16; p. 17.
60 *Why Baptist Are Not Protestants* (pamphlet, publisher and date unknown, nd), p. 4. I do not agree with Lyons' assertion in his title that Baptists are not Protestants. Baptists *are* Protestants in that they emerged out of the 17th century English Separatists, not the Anabaptists.

enhanced, and acceptance is made sure, by a personal, public confession of faith.

> Unconverted members lower the whole tenor of the church. Do what we may, Judas will come in; but let us not invite him . . . To mix up the world with the church, is a crime; it brings with it an awful curse, and acts upon godliness as a blast and a mildew. As you love your Lord, and value men's souls, guard well the entrance into the church.[61]

The *third* requirement is a godly life. This is not speaking of perfection or of the life of a seasoned Christian of twenty-five years. However, there must be evidence, according to 2 Corinthians 5:17, that an individual has become a new creation: old things have passed away and all things are becoming new. Without a changed life and fruits of Christlikeness, no one can join a church of Jesus Christ. The predecessor to Spurgeon at the Metropolitan Tabernacle, John Gill, states it quite well with the following:

> In general, it may be observed, that all such who are of immoral lives. . .and of unsound principles, as to the doctrines of the gospel, are not proper persons to be members of a gospel church; no unclean persons, nor thieves, nor covetous, nor drunkards, nor revilers, nor extortioners, have, or should have any inheritance, part or portion in the kingdom of God. . .; and though there may be such secretly, who creep in unawares, yet when discovered are to be excluded; and such persons, therefore, who are to be put away from a church, as wicked men, and such as walk disorderly, are to be withdrawn from, and such as have imbibed false doctrines, are to be rejected; then most certainly

---

[61] C.H. Spurgeon, *The Sword and Trowel*, "The 1888 Presidential Address" (Pasadena, TX: Pilgrim Publications). This quote is actually two separate quotes taken from the same address.

such are not knowingly to be admitted into. . .a church of Christ, or be at first received into the fellowship of one.[62]

The *fourth* requirement for church membership is baptism. Time and space forbid further deliberation into the who, what, why, and when of baptism. This is a study in and of itself, and one that is sadly neglected in churches today. In spite of this neglect, Acts 2:40 teaches that before a Christian can become a member of a visible church, he or she must be baptized. "The opinion has been held, almost as a theological axiom," writes J.L. Dagg, "that baptism is the door into the church."[63] No baptism, no membership.

The *last* requirement for church membership is an unreserved commitment to the church you are joining. Why join a church if you do not plan to adhere to its doctrinal beliefs, to faithfully worship with its members, to serve in its ministries, to give to its support, and to pray for its leaders, members, and endeavors? Why join a church if, after two weeks, you stop attending and never actively participate in its life? Faithfulness in following Christ demands faithfulness to His visible church. If there is no intention to be faithful and fully committed to the church, there should be no membership.

One reason that there is so much confusion and a lack of power in many churches scattered throughout the world is because they have ceased to maintain purity in their assemblies by forsaking divinely-appointed requirements for membership. They have grown to fear men rather than fearing the holy anger of a righteous God in heaven who said, *"Be holy, for I am holy."* In so doing, they have lost the LORD'S blessing.

---

[62] *Body of Divinity*, vol. II, (Grand Rapids: Baker Book House, 1978), pp. 562-563.
[63] *Manual of Theology*, Second Part, (Harrisburg, VA: Gano Books/Sprinkle Publications, 1982), p. 135.

DISCUSSION FOR CHAPTER FIFTEEN:

1. Discuss John Owen's contrast between the apostolic pattern of receiving church members and modern practices.

2. Review the order of the requirements and discuss whether you think this order is important.

3. What insight into apostolic practice and order does Acts 2:41-42 give us about *"continuing steadfastly"*?

4. Discuss why there is so much confusion and lack of power in churches throughout the world.

16

How is a Christian Admitted into Membership?
&
How is Membership Terminated?

"However, many of those who heard the Word believed;
and the number of the men came to be about five thousand."
(Acts 4:4)

THE APOSTOLIC CHURCH did keep records. That is why we
have the record that 3,000 souls were added to the church on
the day of Pentecost, and 2,000 were added a week or so later.[64]
Because the numbers were so large, the church, of necessity,
certainly kept a roll so that baptized believers in Christ could be
identified with non-believers. We are not told explicitly how
people were received into membership, but an inductive study
of the Scriptures gives us insight and directives. Edmund
Clowney gives us some help with this consideration:

The lists of names in the book of Numbers give evidence of God's
concern to define membership in his people; God's book of life is
the archetype of the earthly register of his people (Ex. 32:32-33;

---

[64] Do not be confused or argumentative regarding the word "about", which is
found in the two accounts. Luke is not avoiding a precise and exact number, but as
Bruce Metzger observes in his *Textual Commentary* (p. 275), it is Luke's favorite way
to express numerical counts taking into consideration the fluid additions,
subtractions, and defections.

Mal. 3:16). A prophetic psalm foresees the recording of Gentile names on the rolls of Zion (Ps. 87:4-6). The names of Euodia, Syntyche and Clement, recognized members of Christ's body at Philippi, are in the book of life, according to Paul (Phil. 4:2-3). Matthias, chosen in the place of Judas, is numbered with the eleven apostles; those who were added to the church were numbered with the disciples, so that total numbers could be set down (Acts 1:15, 26; 2:41; 4:4). Significantly, the first total of three thousand is given in connection with baptism (Acts 2:41).[65]

How, then, can a person be brought into the membership of a visible church? There are *four* ways an individual may become a member of a visible church:

First, by applying for baptism as a new convert. The Great Commission (Matthew 28:18-20) outlines several steps with regard to new converts. The very first step, obviously, is to believe upon Christ as Savior from sin and Lord of your life, which is becoming a disciple, or follower of Jesus. The very first commandment given to a new disciple is to follow Christ in the waters of baptism. When a disciple is baptized, he or she publicly confesses Christ as Lord and Savior. Through baptism, a believer publicly takes the name of Christ upon himself and identifies with Christ the Lord. From that point, the Christian is called to continually live a life of submission to *"whatsoever things"* Christ has taught in His Word. This obedience is in the context of the church and under the ministry of the church. A careful study of the NT reveals that, contrary to popular practice, no one was ever baptized without becoming a member of a church. That which frequently occurs today was unheard of in apostolic times. Baptism is the first way a believer can become a member of a church.

---

[65] *The Church,* Ibid., p. 104.

Second, an individual may become a member of a visible church by transferring a letter of membership from a sister church of like faith and practice. The practice of church members' having letters of commendations goes all the way back to apostolic days. When messengers or members of one church were sent or moved to another location where there was a biblical church, a letter of commendation was sent by the church on their behalf (cf. Acts 18:27). This letter gave assurance that the believer(s), who were most likely unknown to the other church, were in good standing with Christ's people and were not under discipline. If a person is a member of a visible church and moves, a letter of transfer can be sent to verify the status of "good standing" in the previous church.

Third, there are some unusual situations and circumstances in which a person has been converted and baptized without becoming a member of a visible church. In such cases, after a thorough examination by the pastors and elders, a person may be brought into membership by testimony of gospel conversion and baptism, without having a letter from another church.

The **fourth** way in which one may join a church had to do with a person who has been excommunicated from a church because of unrepentant, flagrant sin. When such a person manifests *biblical repentance*, he or she may be restored to membership and fellowship. If the church where the believer was excommunicated is another church, communication needs to be established between the excommunicating church and the restoring church. This allows for the records of both churches to be updated, for the testimony of Christ to be maintained, for the reputation of the disciplined person to be restored, and for rejoicing to take place.

It is advisable that the candidate for membership be knowledgeable concerning the information found in this study. Some churches have membership classes, while others require the applicant to do specific studies and then to meet with the elders for a final interview before being made a member. Either method is beneficial in making a strong visible church. [66]

How can membership within a visible church be terminated? There are also *four* ways a Christian may have his or her membership terminated in a visible church:

By letter. A member may, upon request, receive a letter of commendation and dismissal from his church. He or she may use this letter to unite with another church of like faith and practice, thus not passing out of church relations, but transferring from one congregation to another.

By excommunication. When a church exercises its lawful authority of discipline upon a member who refuses to repent of open and flagrant sin, it severs fellowship. This is extremely serious; in fact, the Apostle Paul describes it as being delivered *"to Satan for the destruction of the flesh"* (1 Corinthians 5:5). When this action is taken, the connection with the church is dissolved.

By death. The death of a member, of course, dissolves the relationship, transferring him or her from the assembly on earth to that in heaven, from the church militant to the church triumphant.

By voluntary withdrawal. Church membership is voluntary, both in coming in and going out. Unless a member is under discipline, he or she may withdraw and leave at any time. It must be noted that a great danger is that sometimes a member

---

[66] Membership Class Notes are available at **www.hbcshreveport.com**. You can download and print out one set for your own personal study. If you desire to use these in a class setting please contact the church for more information.

will withdraw and never associate with another assembly. *Saving Christianity cannot be divorced from the church; the NT knows nothing of a churchless Christianity! To think lightly of the church is to think lightly of Christ, who died for the church.* To leave one visible church without joining another oftentimes, though not always, demonstrates an empty profession.

Another problem is that, occasionally, a member withdraws because he or she anticipates being formally disciplined. Such a person must seriously consider that the discipline of the LORD cannot be avoided. God is not mocked (Galatians 6:7). He or she may escape the discipline of the church, but the discipline of the LORD is inescapable. *'For we know Him who said, 'Vengeance is Mine, I will repay,' says the Lord. And again, 'The LORD will judge His people.' It is a fearful thing to fall into the hands of the living God"* (Hebrews 10:30-31).

In conclusion, please read carefully the following quote by Edward Hiscox. It is succinct and drives to the very heart of what a believer's attitude should be in relation to this subject of biblical churchmanship. May God give us hearts to heed all the things that have been presented in this study.

> It is sometimes said that a church is a voluntary society. This is true in a sense and only with an explanation. It is true that no external force or authority can compel the relation of membership to be formed or dissolved. The church can compel no one to unite with it, nor can the individual oblige the body to receive him. But it is not true that it is a matter merely optional and indifferent whether or not a believer identifies himself with the household of faith. He is under moral obligation to do that. It is for his own spiritual good to do it. It is one of the appointed means of grace. The church needs his presence and influence, and the cause of truth is

furthered by a combination of Christian influence and effort. All are under law to Christ and are bound by sacred obligation to obey and please Him. He has ordained that His followers should associate themselves in those brotherhoods of faith and affection. *A church, therefore, is more than a voluntary society. It is a society under law to Christ. Church membership, therefore, becomes a question of grave moment and should be carefully studied and well understood.*[67]

DISCUSSION FOR CHAPTER SIXTEEN:

1. How do we know that the apostolic church kept records?

2. What are the four ways an individual may become a member of a visible church? Which one is the most applicable to you?

3. Discuss the four ways a Christian may have his or her membership terminated.

4. In light of 1 Corinthians 5, why is excommunication so serious?

5. What are the potential dangers of voluntary withdrawal?

6. In what sense is it true and in what sense is it *not* true that a church is a voluntary society?

7. What does Hiscox mean when he says, "All are under law to Christ and are bound by sacred obligations to obey and please Him"?

8. If you are *not* a member of a visible New Testament church, what do you believe Christ would have you to do?

9. If you are a member of a visible NT church, have you given thanks to the triune God for the benefits that you have received from it? What are you most thankful for?

10. If you are a member of a visible NT church, in what ways are you seeking to be a blessing in it and to serve Christ through it?

---

[67] Edward Hiscox, *Principles and Practices for Baptist Churches*, p. 80.

17

WHEN IS IT RIGHT TO LEAVE A CHURCH AND HOW SHOULD IT BE DONE?

"Let all things be done decently and in order."
(1 Corinthians 14:40)

WHY SHOULD WE EVEN consider this subject? Since this book has been of a positive nature, should not negatives be avoided? Simply put, there are numerous reasons why this subject should be considered:

1) because people do in reality leave churches;

2) because some people leave churches in ways that are often disagreeable to the Word of God. They cause hurt and confusion. They place stumbling blocks in the paths of believers and unbelievers and bring reproach upon the Word of God, God Himself, and His church. They disrupt the fellowship and gospel communion between churches;

3) because the Scriptures are sufficient to address this issue;

4) because just as we joined the church to the glory of God, we want to leave the church to the glory of God (1 Corinthians 10:31);

5) because the triune God is worthy for us to behave in a godly manner in our leaving (Ephesians 3:21).

What is meant by the expression "to leave a church"? It is not just going home after a Lord's Day worship service or a midweek prayer meeting. To leave a church in a godly manner means to depart correctly (for the right reasons) through proper resignation of membership. Many times the event of one's leaving a church is heart-wrenching, deeply soul-troubling, and can be accompanied by negative effects on the body. Usually, church constitutions or denominational books of church order contain directions as to how this can be done righteously.

Historically, Baptists have always held to the position of voluntary church membership. They do not believe that the children of all believers must, of necessity, and involuntarily, become members of the church through infant baptism. While it is obligatory for all believers to be baptized and to join a local assembly, it is never forced upon them either to become or to remain members. I assert that those Christians who have not submitted themselves to and obeyed the NT teaching on biblical churchmanhip have not enjoyed, nor can they enjoy, the full and rich blessings of Christ, who is the Head of the church. Leaving is not an end unto itself. If you still maintain your confession of Christ as your Lord and Savior, and if you leave one visible church, it is expected that you will go to another visible church (i.e., assembly, body of Jesus Christ) and join it.

WHAT ARE SOME BIBLICAL GROUNDS FOR LEAVING A CHURCH?

Reasons for leaving a church are numerous. Many are without biblical foundation and warrant. The only biblical grounds for a person's leaving a church are:

1) when a church departs from the gospel and the preaching thereof;

2) when a church embraces and teaches heresy;

3) when a church tolerates open and scandalous sin in the church leadership or membership and refuses to deal with it via biblical church discipline;

4) when a church changes doctrinal positions not consistent with the church's original Confession of Faith, doctrines, or practices (e.g., becoming paedobaptistic or charismatic);

5) when a member (who is not under discipline) changes his major doctrinal position from that of his church;

6) when a member is providentially moved to another location far away from his or her present church (e.g., job relocation where there is another good church; Christian service to another church or country; marriage to a Christian in another church; etc.).

WHAT ARE SOME REASONS WHY YOU SHOULD *NOT* LEAVE A CHURCH?

Many and sad are the reasons people often leave churches. It is unfortunate that many disregard scriptural admonitions and choose to carnally go their own way and do their own thing. Listed below are some reasons why you should *not* leave a church:

• Because you reject hard sayings and teachings of the Holy Bible and their implications (John 6:36-71, esp. v. 60, where Christ's disciples complained of His "hard" sayings). Other examples include biblical doctrines that are not palatable, instruction on church discipline, penetrating sermons, Sunday School lessons that seek to address today's lawless practices, pastoral counsel that people do not want to hear.

- Because you do not get your way about non-salvific matters (Philippians 2:3). People often make idols of their own ideas or desires. The church vote did not go the way you wanted. The pastors/elders or deacons did not do what you thought was best. "I don't like the way they did it. . ." However, you must remember that the church is not about "you." The church is *all* about Christ!

- Because you are unwilling to deal with personal sin when confronted (Matthew 18:15-17).

- Because you will *not* work out personal differences with another brother or sister in a biblical manner (Philippians 4:2). Notice how carefully our Baptist forefathers addressed this issue:

> No church members, upon any offence taken by them, having performed their duty required of them toward the person they are offended at, ***ought to disturb any church order, or absent themselves from the assemblies of the church, or administration of any ordinances***, upon the account of such offence at any of their fellow members, ***but to wait upon Christ, in the further proceeding of the church***. (emphasis added)[68]

NOTE: Learn to work through difficulties with brethren in a biblical manner. Do not run away to another church. You will only carry your "dirty laundry" with you, see your problems resurface or worsen, and pollute the new church you attend.

---

[68] *The London Baptist Confession of Faith of 1689*, (26:13).

- Because you are under church discipline and you refuse to repent of flagrant sins or doctrines and teachings that caused scandal, division, and offenses (see Romans 16:17-19).

- Because you fail to live the way you should live within the covenant church community and before a watching world (Colossians 3:12-16). You have allowed your heart to grow cold and, when you do so, the cares of the world usurp the rightful place of Christ in your life and heart.

- Because you love the world more than Christ (2 Timothy 4:9-10) and you wish to return to the things that temporarily gratify the flesh.

- Because you get angry and reject exhortations. This often occurs when fellow church members carry out exhortations and admonitions through mutual ministry (1 Thessalonians 5:14) or when pastors caution members of carelessness they observe.

- Because the church does not have all the "programs" you want. Activities and programs, which can create "busyness" to entertain or occupy children or teens, can easily deter people from the authentic purpose of the church.

- Because the worship or preaching does *not* meet your "felt" needs. Society today is so sensory-oriented and emotionally driven that objective truth is often overrun by subjective feelings.

NOTE: The full-orbed exposition and declaration of the whole counsel of God's Word is more important than people or their desire for programs or their "felt" needs! A consistent expository ministry will *eventually* meet all "felt" needs.

- Because you are not a true Christian (1 John 2:19). If you are a church member and come to believe you are not a true Christian, the thing to do is *not* leave the church, but repent and believe the gospel. Let the pastor(s) know of your conversion, be baptized as a believer, and then truly join the church.

HOW THEN SHOULD YOU LEAVE A CHURCH WHEN YOU HAVE BIBLICAL GROUNDS?

Before we consider this section, there are three presuppositions that are indicative of all Christians. These three must regulate all that we think and do. They are the following:

i. Christians are genuinely loving (John 13:33-34);

ii. Christians are experientially and practically holy (1 Peter 1:15-16);

iii. Christians earnestly rejoice in Christ and want to please Him (1 Peter 1:8).

With these three indicatives in mind, how should a Christian leave a church when there is biblical warrant to do so? Listed below are several ways a believer should leave a church:

- With the Word of Christ *dwelling* in your heart and directing all your actions (Colossians 3:15-17);

- With love to God and your brothers and sisters in Christ *characterizing* your exodus (1 Corinthians 13:1-8);

- With the fruit of the Holy Spirit *exuding* from your person (Galatians 5:22-23);

- With the mind of Christ *governing* your attitude (Philippians 2:3-4, especially see the context of vv. 1-12);

- With the wisdom that is from above *controlling* your conduct (James 3:13-18);

- With a forgiving spirit, void of bitterness, *attending* your exit (Ephesians 4:32; Hebrews 12:14-16);

- With a sacrificial heart *beating* within you towards your brethren who remain (1 John 3:16-18);

- With a face-to-face farewell (3 John 13-14).

CLOSING SUGGESTIONS

May I make several suggestions regarding leaving a church?

1) Seek counsel before deciding to leave, especially from your pastors and elders (Proverbs 11:14, 15:22, 24:6);

2) Do unto others as you would have them do unto you; in other words, leave as you would like to be left (Matthew 7:12);

3) Clean up any unresolved matters before you leave (Ephesians 4:1-3);

4) Leave in a way that does not cause confusion or division after you leave (1 Corinthians 14:33);

5) Leave in such a way that you can be heartily commended to another church (Philemon 12 and all the verses that deal with commendation);

6) Leave in such a way that your attitude and conduct will not hinder your coming back;

7) Upon leaving, do *not* think or speak evilly of those who remain (1 Corinthians 13:4-7, especially v. 5);

8) Make sure you know where you are going. Do not leave without a plan as to which church you will go. Many leave and stop going to church altogether. Again, I remind you that the NT knows nothing of a churchless Christianity!

CONCLUSION:

Many, because they do not get their way about matters, or because they get their feelings hurt, or because they do not like what is being preached and taught, or a host of other reasons, carelessly and callously leave churches. They are *not* under the government and rule of the Holy Scriptures and really do not desire to be. They cause division and hurt feelings, say harsh things after they leave, seek to pull others away, and have little concern for the testimony of Christ in the world. May we not be like them.

There are situations when it is right to leave a church. If, in the providence of God, one must leave a church, let it be done in a manner that will bring glory to God and do good to others. May we walk humbly before the triune God and others, learn to work out differences in a righteous fashion, esteem our brethren better than ourselves, bear with one another, forgive one another, root out any bitterness, let go of grudges, and love Christ with all our ransomed powers! Remember that visible churches are central to all of the redemptive purposes of God in Christ Jesus. Christ walks among them (see Revelation 1:13 & 20). Let us do all that we can to make the church more wholesome, effective, productive, vibrant, and attractive.

DISCUSSION FOR CHAPTER SEVENTEEN:

1. Why is it necessary to consider the subject of leaving a church? (Give 5 reasons)

2. What is meant by "leaving a church"?

3. List and discuss the six biblical grounds for leaving a church.

4. What are some reasons people should *not* leave a church?

5. Discuss the three presuppositions that are indicative of all Christians.

6. When it becomes necessary, what are the several ways believers should leave a church?

7. Go over the *eight* suggestions given that one should follow before making a decision to leave a church.

8. Have you seen people wrongfully leave a church? What effects did this have upon you? The church?

9. If you are a member of a church, what do you think you can do to make it more wholesome, effective, productive, vibrant, and attractive?

18

Thoughts Upon the Church from Those Who've Gone Before

". . . he being dead stills speaks."
(Hebrews 11:4c)

"Anyone who cuts themselves off from the Church and is joined to an adulteress is separated from the promises of the Church, and anyone who leaves the Church of Christ behind cannot benefit from the rewards of Christ. Such persons are strangers, outcasts, and enemies. You cannot have God as father unless you have the Church as mother."
-Cyprian, bishop of Carthage (*Corpus Christianorum*, vol. 3, pp. 5-7; martyred in AD 258)

"The Church is the bride which Christ won for Himself at the price of His own blood. Unity is its outstanding characteristic, the bond which holds it together being mutual charity, and the schisms which split it asunder are just as pernicious and blameworthy as the heresies which distort its faith. The Church is . . . spread throughout the whole world; it is indestructible and eternal, the pillar and ground of the truth."
-John Chrysostom (*Homilies on Ephesians*, sermon 11. He was known as "Golden-mouth" and was noted for preaching expositorily through entire books of the Bible. The only book

that Calvin published in Geneva, apart from his own, was a French translation of selected homilies of Chrysostom.)

"At all times and for all pious people the house or temple of God is the place where God is worshiped. For God can be said truly to dwell where people worship Him in truth and to dwell particularly where those who are faithful come together."
-Martin Luther (*Works*, vol.5, p. 142)

"The Lord esteems the communion of his church so highly that he counts as a traitor and apostate from Christianity anyone who arrogantly [refuses to join or] leaves any Christian society, provided it cherishes the true ministry of the Word and sacraments."
-John Calvin (*Institutes of the Christian Religion*, 2:10-12)

"Howbeit, the Scripture doth in general represent the kingdom or church of Christ to consist of persons called *saints*, separated from the world, . . .That, whereas *regeneration* is expressly required in the gospel to give a right and privilege unto an entrance into the church . . .John 3:3, Titus 3:5, whereby that kingdom of His is distinguished from all other kingdoms in and of the world, unto an interest wherein never any such thing was required, it must of necessity be something better, more excellent, and sublime than any thing the laws and polities of men pretend unto or prescribe."
-John Owen (*Works*, vol. 15 "The Nature of a Gospel Church"; p. 14)

"And Christ delights and rejoices in the **beauty of the church,** the beauty which he hath put upon her: her Christian graces are 'ornaments of great price in his sight' (1 Peter 3:4)."
-Jonathan Edwards (*Sermons and Discourses, 1743-1758*; p. 180)

"The Lord Jesus is the head of the Church, which is composed of all His true disciples, and in Him is invested supremely all power for its government. According to His commandment, Christians are to associate themselves into particular societies or churches; and to each of these churches He hath given needful authority for administering that order, discipline, and worship which He hath appointed. The regular officers of a Church are Bishops or Elders, and Deacons."

-**James P. Boyce**, founder & first President of The Southern Baptist Theological Seminary (*Abstract of Principles*, article XIV. The Church)

"The Church is left in the world still that she may bring out the rest of God's elect that are still hidden in the caverns and strongholds of sin. If God had willed it, He might have brought out all His children by the mere effort of His own power, without the use of any instrumentality. He might have sent His grace into each individual heart in some such miraculous manner as He did in the heart of Saul, when he was going toward Damascus; but he hath not chosen to do so. He, who hath taken the Church to be his spouse and His bride, has chosen to bring men to Himself by means; and thus it is, through God's using the Church, her ministers, her children, her works, her sufferings, her prayers,—through making these the means of the increase of His spiritual kingdom, she proves her right to take to herself the title of mother."

-**Charles Haddon Spurgeon** (*Metropolitan Tabernacle Pulpit*, "The Church A Mother"; vol. 48; p. 194)

Reader, are your thoughts of the church lower than these great and mightily used servants of Christ? Are you wiser and more enlightened than they? Let the Word of God and Christ's love constrain you. Contemplate these extraordinary Christological truths:

- the cosmos of light, glory, and love Christ left to come into this world of darkness, shame, and hatred;

- the divine distance Jesus traveled from glory to earth to become the God-man, one with us;

- the lowly position He assumed, as a servant with no reputation;

- the humiliation He experienced, being *"despised and rejected of men"*;

- the contradiction of lying sinners against Himself He endured;

- the shame He despised being stripped naked, spat upon, and mocked in Pilate's judgment hall;

- the loneliness Jesus felt when all but one of His apostles (John) turned from Him;

- the grief He bore as the thorns stabbed His brow and the nails pierced His hands and feet;

- the painful agony He suffered on the cross as His body was broken;

- the abandonment He faced when the Father forsook Him in His most trying hours;

- the spiritual devastation Jesus underwent when the Father poured out His wrath upon His Son for our sins;

- the disbelief He encountered, even from His apostles, at His resurrection from the dead;

- the hallelujahs He received from the heavenly hosts as He ascended into heaven;

- the scars He now bears in His glorified body from "the five bleeding wounds received on Calvary";

- the reward of His soul's travail that He won—the redemption of His bride;

- and the crown of everlasting honor that He forever wears upon His brow.

The Baptist hymnist, Thomas Kelly, wrote:

> *The Head that once was crowned with thorns*
> *is crowned with glory now;*
> *A royal diadem adorns*
> *the mighty Victor's brow.*
>
> *The cross He bore is life and health,*
> *though shame and death to Him;*
> *His people's hope, His people's wealth,*
> *their everlasting theme.*

What was the driving motivation that caused our Savior, the Lord of glory, to endure such condescension and humiliation for sinners, as these extraordinary Christological truths reveal? It was love—*"Christ loved the church and gave Himself for it."* Samuel J. Stone, in his great hymn, "The Church's One Foundation," expresses it so well:

The church's one foundation is Jesus Christ her Lord;
She is his new creation by water and the Word:
From heav'n he came and sought her to be his holy bride;
With his own blood he bought her and for her life he died.

'Mid toil and tribulation, and tumult of her war,
She waits the consummation of peace forevermore;
Till with the vision glorious her longing eyes are blest,
And the great church victorious shall be the church at rest.

If you have found a faithful church, in which to worship and serve, bless the triune God for it, pray for your pastor(s), and give yourself afresh to its labors. If you have yet to join yourself to a visible body of Christ, search for the nearest church that meets the descriptive qualities presented in this book, join it, and implement biblical churchmanship with all the ransomed ability of a sinner saved by grace *alone*, through faith *alone*, in Christ *alone*. Jesus loves the church and so should you. By the grace of God, may you love her with the same intensity and fervor as He!

❦

Some Other Titles from Solid Ground

In addition to *Jesus Loves the Church and So Should You*, Solid Ground Christian Books has reprinted several volumes from the Puritan era, such as the following:

The Complete Works of Thomas Manton (in 22 volumes)

A Body of Divinity by Archbishop James Ussher

An Exposition of Hebrews by William Gouge

A Short Explanation of Hebrews by David Dickson

An Exposition of the Epistle of Jude by Thomas Jenkyn

A Commentary on the New Testament by John Trapp

Gospel Sonnets by Ralph Erskine

Heaven Upon Earth by James Janeway

The Marrow of True Justification by Benjamin Keach

The Travels of True Godliness by Benjamin Keach

The Redeemer's Tears Wept Over Lost Souls by John Howe

Commentary on the Second Epistle of Peter by Thomas Adams

The Christian Warfare by John Downame

An Exposition of the Ten Commandments by Ezekiel Hopkins

The Harmony of the Divine Attributes by William Bates

The Communicant's Companion by Matthew Henry

The Secret of Communion with God Matthew Henry

View at www.solid-ground-books.com

Call us at 205-443-0311

CPSIA information can be obtained
at www.ICGtesting.com
Printed in the USA
FFOW02n1013110516
23973FF